Even More Stories and Lessons on Feng Shui

又再笑談風水

風水

JOEY YAP

又再笑談風水

Even More Stories and Lessons on Feng Shui

First Edition July 2008

The author can be reached at:

Mastery Academy of Chinese Metaphysics Sdn. Bhd. (611143-A)
19-3, The Boulevard, Mid Valley City,
59200 Kuala Lumpur, Malaysia.
Tel : +603-2284 8080
Fax : +603-2284 1218
Email : info@masteryacademy.com
Website : www.masteryacademy.com

Published by JY Books Sdn. Bhd. (659134-T)

INDEX – EVEN MORE STORIES AND LESSONS

又再笑談風水

III

又再笑談風水

PREFACE

If you mention the word 'Feng Shui' to anyone these days, chances are you'll no longer receive a blank look. The odds are likely that you'll receive an enthusiastic "expert" Feng Shui quick tip in return. It seems that anyone can be a Feng Shui professional nowadays. While that should make me happy, in a sense, because it is certainly encouraging that more people are taking to Feng Shui more than ever before, it also makes me worried.

At the risk of sounding a bit like a snooty Feng Shui elitist, of which I assure you I'm not, I must admit that the popularity of the 3-minute Instant Feng-Shui-in-A-Cup troubles me.

It is absolutely right that Feng Shui should be made available to everyone; in fact, as a teacher, that has been one of my primary goals. However, it should be authentic Feng Shui that's available to everyone. And it's this spread of what I call 'Pop Feng Shui' that gives me pause.

For that purpose, Even More Stories and Lessons in Feng Shui was created. The previous two books in this series, Stories and Lessons in Feng Shui and More Stories and Lessons in Feng Shui seemed to have touched a chord among readers both new and not-so-new to Feng Shui. I was heartened by the response to those books as it indicated a thirst for genuine knowledge among Feng Shui enthusiasts and the merely curious.

Even More Stories and Lessons in Feng Shui continues in the same vein as its predecessors, offering a collection of stories, essays, and anecdotes about my personal experiences with Feng Shui. It doesn't claim to offer you a comprehensive, thorough guide to all things Feng Shui, but it does aim to clear away the cobwebs of superstition and fallacies that hang over Feng Shui and practically all fields of Chinese Metaphysics.

In other words, I invite you to step into my world in order to make some sense of Feng Shui and how it can relate to yours.

There is no particular or 'right' way to read this book. Just as Feng Shui itself is a meandering, exploratory practice, so should your experience be with this book; pick it up and turn to any chapter that strikes your fancy. One might take you deep into the unchartered territories of unexplored lands in India, where I did a Feng Shui consult of the external landforms for a client, while another might take you into the mysterious universe of Qi Men Dun Jia, a discipline in Chinese Metaphysics that was heavily used in Chinese warfare during ancient times due to its precise calculations of time and space.

又再笑談風水

Aside from some of the more practical stories on Feng Shui and its many uses and applications, which urge you to try some simple techniques for yourself while cautioning you to keep in mind context and relevance, as well as levels of expertise, there are also stories and essays that focus on BaZi (Chinese Astrology) and the historical roots and contexts of schools of thought within Feng Shui.

A "Dear Feng Shui Master" chapter compiles some questions with common elements from readers of my previous media columns in the hopes that the answers may be of use for those with similar concerns. And as mentioned earlier, one story takes you to the wild heartlands of India, while another takes you to the height of opulence in Dubai. This will hopefully allow you to see Feng Shui for what it is – not armchair philosophy for the idle and privileged, but as a real, hands-on, often adventurous romp through the world.

If I sound a touch too enthusiastic, it's because I am – there's no point pretending otherwise and persuading you to believe that I'm neutral when it comes to Feng Shui. I'm not; I'm quite happily biased in its favour, in fact, but not to stress its overarching superiority or anything silly and superficial like that. It's only to emphasize its potency and effectiveness when applied correctly, responsibly, and with respect to its history and traditions – what it has is the ability to allow you to experience a fuller, richer, and more expansive life.

And I think we could all do with a little bit of that, don't you think?

I present to you Even More Stories and Lessons in Feng Shui and trust that you'll find your journey into the world of Feng Shui and Chinese Metaphysics to be every bit as enlightening and enriching as you'd hoped.

Joey Yap
Australia, June 2008

Author's personal website: www.joeyyap.com | www.fengshuilogy.com
Academy website:
www.masteryacademy.com | www.masteryjournal.com | www.maelearning.com

又再笑談風水

MASTERY ACADEMY
OF CHINESE METAPHYSICS™

At www.masteryacademy.com, you will find some useful tools to ascertain key information about the Feng Shui of a property or for study of Astrology.

The Joey Yap Flying Star Calculator can be utilized to plot your home or office Flying Star chart. To find out your personal best directions, use the 8 Mansions Calculator. To learn more about your personal Destiny, you can use the Joey Yap BaZi Ming Pan Calculator to plot your Four Pillars of Destiny – you just need to have your date of birth (day, month, year) and time of birth.

For more information about BaZi, Xuan Kong or Flying Star Feng Shui, or if you wish to learn more about these subjects with Joey Yap, logon to the Mastery Academy of Chinese Metaphysics website at **www.masteryacademy.com**

The Real Story on Feng Shui

When someone mentions Feng Shui to you, you probably see a vision of bamboo flutes and wind chimes, think of Ba Gua mirrors or perhaps recall something about lucky frogs. The reputation of Feng Shui as a respected science and art has taken a beating over the last few years. Some people consider it superstition, others consider it old wives' tales and with the number of luck-enhancing items and fortune trinkets on the market, more and more people probably think of Feng Shui as psychobabble at best, nonsense at worse.

又再笑談風水

I am glad to have this opportunity, through my writings, to share with all of you my knowledge and research on Classical Feng Shui and hopefully, put this highly credible field of classical study in proper perspective. I intend, in these pieces, to broach the topic of this classical Chinese science in a practical yet informative manner with the sincere aim of clearing up much of the mystery surrounding Feng Shui, dispelling the myths, separating the fact from superstition (indeed, fiction) while showing you how you can successfully apply Classical Feng Shui with measurable results to your home.

I realise some of the information I present may be completely new to some readers, especially if you have only been exposed to what I call New Age Feng Shui all this time. The best approach therefore is to keep an open mind and I will endeavour to help you better understand this fascinating and empowering science.

What Is Classical Feng Shui Really All About?

If there is one certainty I can be assured of each time I undertake a speaking engagement, it is to be approached by someone asking me if they have "bought the wrong cures" or "placed the wrong items" in their home or office, or who are puzzled as to why none of my recommendations or suggestions include something they can buy or place in a certain corner or direction.

This underlines the problem with Feng Shui today – there is a clear lack of understanding regarding Classical Feng Shui and what the practice of Feng Shui entails. Commercialisation, while bringing the concept of Feng Shui to the 21st-century masses, has also conveniently left out a lot of the genuine information, in the name of 'getting it to the masses.' I am a firm believer that 'the secrets of the Heavens' (the term used to describe Feng Shui during the Ming and Qing Dynasties) should be shared and available to everyone, and I certainly do not subscribe to diluting or, for that matter, oversimplifying the information.

Therefore, we must first go back to basics and ask the crucial question: what is Feng Shui?

The answer to this question does depend, to some degree, on whether you are talking about New Age Feng Shui or Classical Feng Shui. Most Feng Shui practitioners today fall into two loose categories: the New Age practitioners, and the

又再笑談風水

Classical practitioners. New Age Feng Shui leans heavily towards symbolism and the placement of Chinese cultural items or good fortune cures. New Age Feng Shui is rather all-embracing, and as a result, many New Age practices, like Space Clearing and Dousing, have ostensibly become a part of Feng Shui practices.

However, in actual fact, there is no historical, theoretical, empirical or evidential basis for New Age Feng Shui or the symbolic objects that are frequently recommended as part of the practice of New Age Feng Shui.

Everything in modern-day science, as we understand it, is drawn from basic science. So for example, someone who posits a new theory must premise it on existing knowledge, such as Newton's Law. This is no different in Feng Shui. All the different schools of practice, such as San Yuan, San He, Xuan Kong, Flying Stars, and Eight Mansions, have their origins in ancient classical texts. The newer practices do not. Therefore, concepts like Space Clearing and the Eight Aspirational Directions, and Symbolisms are in fact modern practices that do not derive any of their basis or theories from the classical texts and literatures on Feng Shui.

The Chinese categorized their study of Metaphysics into five distinct classes known as the Chinese Five Arts (Wu Shu 五術). Feng Shui falls under the banner of Physiognomy, the

science of observing and understanding the living environment through applying formulas and calculations to the living environment to assess the potential and possible outcomes for a person living in a particular property.

Classical Feng Shui began its life as Kan Yu about 1,500 years ago and was used primarily for burial sites. Today, this particular field of practice is known as Yin Feng Shui. Only towards the end of the Qing Dynasty did the term 'Feng Shui' become more commonplace. Like many of the Chinese Metaphysical sciences, Classical Feng Shui is a field of study that was well-documented and there are numerous texts on Classical Feng Shui theories and techniques.

Classical Feng Shui's most obvious distinguishing feature is that all the schools are premised upon four primary aspects – Residents, Time, Building and Environment. They do not have references to items or products but focus solely on the use of DIRECTION and LOCATION with reference to the above four factors.

The objective of Feng Shui is to harness the Qi in the environment to support us in our endeavours.

The objective of Feng Shui is to harness the Qi in the environment to support us in our endeavours. It is a science for assessing the quality of a person's life by looking at their living environment and seeking to improve that quality of life by tapping into the natural energies – the Qi – of that environment.

Feng Shui is not Chinese culture. Classical Feng Shui has nothing to do with the art of placement or symbols or even living in harmony with nature. It has nothing to do with your hair colour or the pendants or crystals you wear and certainly, it has nothing to do with what colour your house or your toilet door is.

The application of Feng Shui also has no religious elements or beliefs, contrary to popular misconception. Again, this is the problem caused by New Age Feng Shui, which deploys as part of its practice a lot of the typical Taoist symbols and deities, such as the Happy Buddha or the Trio of Fu Lu Shou. It also stems from the fact that in the early 1900s, the practitioners of Feng Shui were usually also religious practitioners or people associated with the local temple. There is absolutely not one iota of reference to the need for such items as part of the practice of Feng Shui. The Ba Gua, the He Tu, the Luo Shu numbers, and the Five Elements, all which form the backbone of the practice of Feng Shui, have no religious implications.

The application of Feng Shui also has no religious elements or beliefs, contrary to popular misconception.

Making Classical Feng Shui work for you

又再笑談風水

When you apply classical Feng Shui to your home or office, you are looking at harnessing the Qi that is already present in your environment and then making changes within your property to ensure the Qi supports you in your life's goals. Many people have the idea of Feng Shui as a magic wand that would make their lives better overnight. In truth, Feng Shui is a goal-oriented science. What do you want to achieve in life? What are your aspirations for the year to come? The next 10 years? The end game?

In answering these questions, a Feng Shui consultant is essentially looking to determine if the place in which you live or work is 'with you or against you'. Besides supporting the individual's aspirations in life, Feng Shui is also extremely useful for the strategic planning of one's life. Through Feng Shui, it is possible to assess the outcome that may culminate as a result of living in a particular property. This is because Qi is cyclical in nature and the influences in your living environment can be calculated based on formulas. By knowing the potential pitfalls and the highs and the lows that are likely to come, and then matching this information with that derived from a person's BaZi or Destiny chart, it is truly possible to plan for the future and use Feng Shui to assist you in achieving your life goals!

又再笑談風水

Classical or New Age?

The main goal of the many articles I write on Classical Feng Shui is simply to educate and inform, and to help people understand the difference between New Age and Classical Feng Shui.

Many people aren't aware of the difference between these two methods of Feng Shui that are advocated today. Many times when the word "Feng Shui" is mentioned, people will quickly assume it's about fixing problems in a house by placing an object or item in a specific corner.

Well, if this is your impression of Feng Shui, then chances are you are practicing "New Age" Feng Shui. Classical Feng Shui does not advocate the use of symbols or objects.

This type of Feng Shui taps into the environmental energy (Qi) by using mainly four important factors – environmental features, building (direction and location), residents (birth data) and time. All that is needed for a good Feng Shui is for the residents to tap the Qi. There is no need to enhance or remedy anything.

Environment	Building	Residents	Time

Classical Feng Shui methods include San Yuan 三元, Xuan Kong Da Gua 玄空大卦, Ba Zhai 八宅 and San He 三合 which are all traceable to ancient classical literature. These works are available from libraries and Chinese bookstores and they document the actual form of Feng Shui practices since the Tang Dynasty until the present day. And, believe it or not, none of these words make any references to the use of symbols or objects in the house.

又再笑談風水

Hence, the term for Feng Shui that involves placement of objects and symbols is "New Age" Feng Shui simply because it's really something very new.

I've been asked a number of times by various people about how to harness Qi and more importantly, how they can apply it correctly in their own homes and offices. And of course, as usual, they wanted something very easy to learn and ready for immediate use.

How many people would like a simple solution that will bring about an immense change in the Feng Shui of their property?

Everyone?

Me too. Honestly. I would really love it if Feng Shui were a weekend do-it-yourself project that required nothing more that a couple of screws, a hammer and an electric drill. And possibly with a simple diagram that shows what goes where.

However, the truth of the matter is that Feng Shui, like any science, requires a great deal of study, and is by no means a weekend subject. The various systems of classical Feng Shui – San Yuan, San He, Xuan Kong, Ba Zhai, and the rest are already an indication of the vastness and richness of the knowledge contained within Feng Shui.

But people are always interested in something they can implement "right now" and in obtaining quick answers and quick fixes to problems that they are facing. It's sad that people are willing to trade quality for a quick fix that may not even work effectively.

又再笑談風水

Although there is no such things as a quick fix, the easiest method I can prescribe for you would be the simple Ba Zhai (Eight Mansions) Feng Shui technique. There are many parts to this system – House Gua, Life Gua, Na Jia, and Xuan Kong Water Method – to name a few.

Several distinct ancient classics relate to this particular system of Feng Shui and most of them are pretty sophisticated. The simplest method available to us is the Life Gua method. Your initial starting point for this methodology will be your date of birth. Based on this, we will then ascertain your Life Gua or your Ming Gua 命卦. Each Gua is unique and will indicate your favourable and unfavourable compass directions and locations.

A common mistake among beginners who attempt this method is using the Chinese lunar calendar instead of using the Chinese solar calendar, which is what is used for Feng Shui calculations. The solar calendar is based on the 24 Qi seasons and each year starts on the Western calendar's February 4 (with a variance of one day on either side). February 4 of the Western Gregorian calendar synchronizes with the first day of the Chinese solar calendar.

A primary difference between the Chinese solar and lunar calendars is that the former is based on the position of the Sun while the latter is based on the moon and as such contains an additional month every few years. If you were born before February 4 of any year, use the previous year as your point of reference when calculating your Life Gua. Once you have established your year of birth, refer to the following table for a step-by-step guide to calculating your Life Gua.

Do take note that the males and females have different methods to calculate their Life Gua. Calculate your Ming Gua using the directions shown in the image. These numbers are categorized into two groups: the East and the West Group.

Calculating Your Life Gua (命卦)

FOR MALES	FOR FEMALES
Ascertain your Year of Birth. Make sure you know the cut-off point is **February 4th**.	Ascertain your Year of Birth. Make sure you know the cut-off point is **February 4th**.
• Add up the last two digits of your year of birth. • Reduce it to a single digit . • The result number will be your Life Gua number.	• Add up the last two digits of your year of birth. • Reduce it to a single digit. • For Females, ADD 5 to this digit. • The result number will be your Life Gua number.
Example year of birth: 1954 5 + 4 = 9 10 - 9 = 1	**Example year of birth:** 1974 7 + 4 = 11 1 + 1 = 2 2 + 5 = 7
* For a Male person born (after Feb 4) in 1954, his Life Gua is 1.	* For a Female person born (after Feb 4) in 1974, her Life Gua is 7.

Some clients have asked me why there are no North and South groups. Well, these are just names to demarcate the Greater and Lesser Yin transformation of the Tai Ji. They do not literally represent directions. East Group is the Yang group while the West Group is the Yin. East Group Gua include 1, 3, 4 and 9. Those who are Gua 2, 6, 7, and 8 are West Group Gua.

The graphics on the following table (in "Compass Directions") will give you a quick reference of the Auspicious and Inauspicious compass directions of the East and West Group. Each direction is governed by a star. In the Chinese texts, these are called the "Wandering Stars." Sheng Qi 生氣 (life generating), Tian Yi 天醫 (heavenly doctor), Yan Nian 延年 (longevity) and Fu Wei 伏位 (Stability) are Auspicious stars.

East Group 東命

卦 Gua	生氣 Sheng Qi Life Generating	天醫 Tian Yi Heavenly Doctor	延年 Yan Nian Longevity	伏位 Fu Wei Stability	禍害 Huo Hai Mishaps	五鬼 Wu Gui Five Ghosts	六然 Liu Sha Six Killings	絕命 Jue Ming Life Threatening
坎 Kan 1 Water	South East	East	South	North	West	North East	North West	South West
震 Zhen 3 Wood	South	North	South East	East	South West	North West	North East	West
巽 Xun 4 Wood	North	South	East	South East	North West	South West	West	North East
離 Li 9 Fire	East	South East	North	South	North East	West	South West	North West

West Group 西命

卦 Gua	生氣 Sheng Qi Life Generating	天醫 Tian Yi Heavenly Doctor	延年 Yan Nian Longevity	伏位 Fu Wei Stability	禍害 Huo Hai Mishaps	五鬼 Wu Gui Five Ghosts	六然 Liu Sha Six Killings	絕命 Jue Ming Life Threatening
坤 Kun 2 Earth	North East	West	North West	South West	East	South East	South	North
乾 Qian 6 Metal	West	North East	South West	North West	South East	East	North	South
兌 Dui 7 Metal	North West	South West	North East	West	North	South	South East	East
艮 Gen 8 Earth	South West	North West	West	North East	South	North	East	South East

(An interesting point to note here is that in some references, 'Yan Nian 延年' is written as 'Nian Yen.' This is incorrect as the Chinese texts clearly state 'Yan Nian,' meaning verbatim "Prolonging Years." If you are serious about Feng Shui, the terminology is very important and you need to ensure that you are correct.)

The Inauspicious Stars are Huo Hai 禍害 (Mishaps), Wu Gui 五鬼 (Five Ghosts), Liu Sha 六煞 (Six Killings) and Jue Ming 絕命 (Life Threatening).

Auspicious Star:

生氣 *Sheng Qi* **Life Generating**	天醫 *Tian Yi* **Heavenly Doctor**	延年 *Yan Nian* **Longevity**	伏位 *Fu Wei* **Stability**

Inauspicious Star:

禍害 *Huo Hai* **Mishaps**	五鬼 *Wu Gui* **Five Ghosts**	六煞 *Liu Sha* **Six Killings**	絕命 *Jue Ming* **Life Threatening**

I hope that this has gone some way in explaining the fundamental differences between Classical and New Age Feng Shui. With New Age Feng Shui masquerading as Classical Feng Shui these days, it is easy to become a little sidetracked or confused. Just remember: if it seems too good to be true and requires you to shell out some serious money to buy an 'object' that will miraculously transform your life – it probably IS too good to be true! Also, authentic Feng Shui takes time and effort; so if you're willing to be patient before seeing results, the benefits of Classical Feng Shui will make itself apparent to you.

又再笑談風水

An Ancient Art in Modern Times

It may seem odd for me to discuss the question of 'What is Feng Shui?' but I realized that I sometimes take it for granted that people are aware of and understand all the basics of Feng Shui. I still receive a diversity of views from people on what they think Feng Shui is really all about, some of which are quite amusing. What really took the cake was when someone at a wedding dinner last weekend asked me if I was wearing a Feng Shui watch!

又再笑談風水

The question 'What is Feng Shui' looks on the surface to be a no-brainer. Surely everyone knows what is Feng Shui? Why is there a need to answer this question?

Honestly, in this day and age, the question 'What is Feng Shui' is unlikely to solicit any kind of consistent answer. Everyone has their own interpretation or answer to that question. That is not to say that all those answers are necessarily correct. But at the same time, a definitive answer is not easy in modern times. Why? Because Feng Shui is no longer the same art it was 2000 years ago, when it was known as Kan Yu and was mostly utilized by the Imperial family to select burial grounds and locate capital cities.

Feng Shui has evolved. Today, if you visit the Feng Shui section of a bookstore (sometimes labeled as 'Alternative' or 'Far East Philosophy'), you'll find books on everything from crystal therapy to interior design to space clearing. So you see, the question 'What is Feng Shui' is in fact quite hard to answer.

I prefer to phrase the question in this manner: what is Classical Feng Shui? Classical Feng Shui is first and foremost my term for Feng Shui that is based on, and utilizes, techniques and methods from classical texts on Feng Shui such as *The Green Satchel, Earth Discern Study Truth, Purple White Scripts, Earth Entering Eye,* and *Snow Heart Classics,* just to name a few. Classical Feng Shui is the term I use to encompass both San He and San Yuan Feng Shui, the two original schools of Feng Shui.

Classical Feng Shui is about tapping into the natural energies of the environment or Qi in order to improve your life and achieve your goals. This is achieved through the correct placement of doors and the appropriate location of important areas of your home like the kitchen, bedroom and study within your house based on the natural external environmental features. Natural environmental features here refer to mountain ranges (Long 龍), landform embraces (Sha 砂), water formations (Shui 水), meridian spots (Xue 穴) and tapping into the correct facing directions (Xiang 向).

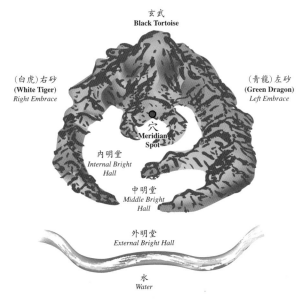

玄武
Black Tortoise

（白虎）右砂
(White Tiger)
Right Embrace

（青龍）左砂
(Green Dragon)
Left Embrace

穴
Meridian Spot

內明堂
Internal Bright Hall

中明堂
Middle Bright Hall

外明堂
External Bright Hall

水
Water

Classical Feng Shui is not about objects or decorative items such as lead crystals, resin dragons or toads. It is not about Bagua mirrors above your main door, Mandarin Ducks on your desk and Fu Dogs at your main gate. Classical Feng Shui is not about space clearing or aromatherapy or wearing certain colours to 'enhance your luck.' Classical Feng Shui is not concerned with landscaping your house with certain type of plants, or the interior decor of your kitchen, or what you put in your handbag, or what number your car plate or house

又再笑談風水

number is. And there's no need to steal soil from your rich neighbour's garden to make a 'wealth vase.' Classical Feng Shui makes absolutely no mention of any of these practices.

These practices are more in line with what I call Pop Feng Shui or New-Age Feng Shui. Pop or New-Age Feng Shui is more about the psychological effect of objects than anything else. It has no consistent principles and its practice is not rooted in any classical theories or ancient texts. Most of the time, Pop Feng Shui or New-Age Feng Shui is a commercialised derivative or watered-down version of certain aspects of Feng Shui sub-systems, or misunderstood nuggets of information from the Yi Jing or traditional Chinese culture. The Eight Life Aspiration system is a good example of Pop or New-Age Feng Shui. This 'system' designates each corner of the house to a particular life aspiration. For example – the North is the Career corner, the Southwest is the Love corner, South the Fame corner and so fourth. This 'system' involves the use of oriental-styled products and Chinese folklore objects to 'enhance' each aspiration within a house.

The 'Eight Life Aspirations' is not a proper Classical Feng Shui system documented in any of the classical texts. It is, like much of Pop or New-Age Feng Shui, a modern and purely commercial invention.

Making an Identification

If you are uncertain as to whether or not something is Classical Feng Shui or some form, version, itineration or off-shoot of pop Feng Shui, there is an easy way to distinguish them.

Typically, all forms of Classical Feng Shui will have the following characteristics:

a) utilizes a Luo Pan for the purposes of acquiring directions

b) involves the analysis of location and direction (North, South, East, West, Northwest, Northeast, Southwest, Southeast)

c) requires the observation of Luan Tou or environmental forms, which include but are not limited to natural mountain shapes, embrace of land by mountains, flow and direction of water

d) takes into account aspects of time

e) considers the residents of the property

f) does NOT require the placement of symbolic items or good luck objects.

g) does NOT involve any spiritual practice or spirituality, or any religious or spiritual activities such as chanting and placement of joss sticks or prayers to deities or figurines

又再笑談風水

If none of these characteristics or features form a part of the technique, method or approach, then it is unlikely to be a part of Classical Feng Shui.

Now, it's tricky these days to sometimes separate the 'pop' from the 'classical' because some Classical Feng Shui practitioners have resorted to adding 'New Age' components to their practice in order to pad their bottom line a little. So they practice Classical Feng Shui, but are not beyond trying to flog you some trinkets or cures.

If you like the psychological aspects of Pop or New Age Feng Shui, or if you find it uplifting or motivational, that is fine. Go ahead and indulge, but be aware that that it is all it is.

I began this with a question: What is Feng Shui? So I would like to end with a question: What is the kind of Feng Shui you would like to utilise? Knowing the answer to this question will enable you to better seek out the right kind of Feng Shui for you and your home. There's a place in this world for all kinds of people, and so by necessity, all kinds of Feng Shui. As long as you know the difference, and you know what you want and what you are getting – that's all that really matters.

Different Schools, Same Goal

Ever since Feng Shui became a popular practice among the masses, it is rare to find a person these days who doesn't know something about Feng Shui, or 'Wind and Water,' as so many people are apt to associate it with. In fact, whatever public knowledge about Feng Shui that exists out there simply scratches the surface of an incredibly deep and profoundly sophisticated science.

The real world of Feng Shui goes far deeper beyond trivial matters like wind chimes and money frogs. It has systems and schools that extend far beyond Flying Stars Feng Shui and Eight Mansions Feng Shui, the two systems that people are most familiar with. It is much more than just about tapping into the energies to improve your love life or to help you get a promotion – in fact, at its most powerful Feng Shui can create Emperors and give birth to Empires. I would like to explain to you the depth that Feng Shui has as a science, and how it leads to and is interlinked with other subjects in Chinese Metaphysics.

The Schools of Feng Shui

To begin to understand Feng Shui, one must first be aware of how it came about. Briefly, Feng Shui originally began as a science of selecting burial grounds (what is known today as Yin House Feng Shui). Also, it wasn't even known as Feng Shui back then. It was known as Kan Yu 堪輿. The name Feng Shui only came into use during the Qing Dynasty. And while it is an ancient science, it is not really THAT old. By most documentary evidence, it is around 1,200 years old and is really only thought to have gained ground and achieved its Renaissance Period during the Tang Dynasty.

Essentially, Feng Shui can be separated into two main schools. Before I delve into the two schools of Feng Shui proper, I must first correct this long-standing error on the two main schools of Feng Shui. It is common today to see books referring to a

COMPASS SCHOOL? FORMS SCHOOL? 'Compass School' and a 'Forms School' of Feng Shui. While it is indeed true that there are two main schools of Feng Shui, they are certainly not distinguished in this manner.

All Feng Shui systems have a core set of principles and theories that are similar – for example, they all refer to the Five Elements, and they all take into account the Four Factors of Residents, Time, Location and Direction. And, they all use a compass or Luo Pan. All schools and systems of Feng Shui involve taking into consideration the surrounding landform. Therefore, it is incorrect to separate Feng Shui systems into either the Compass School or the Forms School.

In actual fact, Feng Shui systems are separated according to whether or not they fall into the Li Qi School, or the Forms School. The Li Qi School focuses on the calculation of Qi through formulas. The Forms School focuses on observation of the physical environment (or landforms) to ascertain the Qi in the area.

The more technical terms for Li Qi and Forms Schools are San Yuan School of Feng Shui or the San He School of Feng Shui. San Yuan and San He are what we call the founding schools of Feng Shui. They are like the Oxford and Cambridge of Feng Shui.

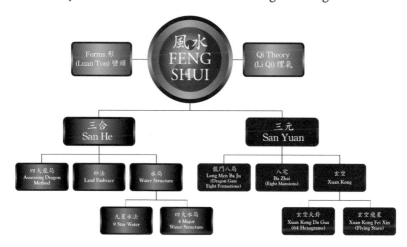

San Yuan and San He Systems

The San Yuan system (San Yuan means 'Three Cycles' in English) is a mathematical model of the Ba Gua that is used to calculate the quality of Qi through time. In San Yuan, Qi is thought to be dynamic but cyclical in nature. All are in a constant state of flux, but within the flux, there are patterns and trends. The objective with San Yuan is to ascertain at which point in time a particular type of Qi at its optimum and to make use of those energies. San Yuan involves updating one's Feng Shui to keep up with the Qi cycle and adopting a dynamic approach to stay in tandem with the changing Qi.

By contrast, San He (which means 'Three Harmony' in English) focuses on the environment – the mountains, the rivers and the landforms - and looks to understand how the environment shapes and creates Qi. It is more focused on finding an optimal or strategic location in which to benefit from the Qi in the environment. San He recognises that Qi is dynamic and changes through time but its premise is on using the unchanging, or Yin, to counter the changing, or the Yang. Landform features, such as mountains and rivers, are considered permanent and unchanging through the times. San He systems do not look to adapt to the changing Qi cycle, but to insulate and outlast any unfavourable periods in the Qi cycle through superior landform.

Both San Yuan and San He take into consideration the Time and Form factors. The difference between the two schools lies in how they prioritise these two factors. San Yuan focuses heavily on the Time factor, while San He focuses more on Forms. From these two founding schools, newer systems have been developed. You see, Feng Shui may be an ancient science, but it is not a science that has been frozen in time.

The San Yuan system has many derivative sub-systems, such as Long Men Ba Ju 龍門八局 (Dragon Gate Eight Formations), Xuan Kong 玄空 (Time and Space School), Xuan Kong Da Gua 玄空大卦 (64 Hexagrams), Xuan Kong Fei Xing 玄空飛星 (Flying Stars) and Ba Zhai 八宅 (Eight Mansions).

Dragon Gate Eight Formations is based on the mathematical model of the Ba Gua and is a study of landform based on intricate calculations. It is, you could say, San Yuan's answer to the San He Landform approach. It is premised on eight sets of Mountain and Water formations and is popular in Taiwan.

又再笑談風水

Xuan Kong incorporates the North Dipper Stars into the mathematical model of the Ba Gua and integrates Landform with Star or Qi calculations. It has spawned two sub-schools of its own, namely, Xuan Kong Da Gua or 64 Hexagrams and Xuan Kong Fei Xing or Flying Stars. In Xuan Kong Da Gua, the 64 Hexagrams are factored into the Time calculations and it is premised on understanding the Star that governs that particular period in time, as well as the Qi pattern of that period, known collectively as the Period Luck (Yuan Yun 元運). It is a highly precise and results-oriented method.

Xuan Kong Fei Xing or Flying Stars and Ba Zhai or Eight Mansions are also systems derived from San Yuan. These are two of the more popular Feng Shui systems used today, especially for Internal Feng Shui. In Flying Stars, a Qi map of the property is derived from calculations and then used to determine the quality of Qi in each sector of the home. Eight Mansions by contrast is about understanding the individual and unique Qi pattern of the House, and then matching the House to the Individual.

A relatively recent addition to this family of systems is a new system known as Qi Men Dun Jia. It is a hybrid system that theoretically is not Feng Shui, but more a divination or probability science. It is mainly used for highly-advanced time selection, such as choosing the right time to install a cure or remove a structure.

Which is better?

People often ask: "Which is more superior, the San Yuan or San He system?" There is no real answer to this question. Each system has its advantages and most practitioners have their pet systems. I prefer not to pursue the debate of which is best, because this is something that has stymied the development of Feng Shui for years. As modern students of this science, I believe the focus should not be on what is best, but on what works in the given circumstances.

In any case, ultimately both San Yuan and San He have common denominators – they all agree that the factor of Time must always be considered and that Landforms cannot be ignored. They are both premised on a mathematical model of the Ba Gua, and both make use of the Five Element theory and are firmly rooted in the concept of Yin and Yang. As well, both San Yuan and San He have one goal in common: the best way to harness Qi in the environment to support one's goals and objectives in life.

Going Beyond Feng Shui

Classical Feng Shui practitioners in the ancient days functioned almost like Imperial advisors. Their roles spanned not just Feng Shui, but military tactics, diplomacy, international affairs and relations, recruitment (hiring of advisors and staff for the Emperor), health, and even economics (by way of advising the Emperor on the best time for harvesting and planting of crops). Accordingly, their skills in the old days encompassed a wide range of Chinese Metaphysical subjects. They were expected to be able to master not just Feng Shui, but Astrology, Divination, Face Reading and Palmistry.

Today, it is no different. In-house Feng Shui Masters to business tycoons and corporate bigwigs give advice not only on matters relating to Feng Shui, but on the timing of business ventures and contract-signing, employee placement and even, economic forecasting. As such, they are often highly-skilled practitioners of not just Feng Shui, but BaZi or Purple Star Astrology, Divination and sometimes even Face Reading. Successful practice of Feng Shui therefore demands substantial cross-disciplinary knowledge and is in fact a multi-disciplinary field. It is much more than mere interior decoration, 'being one and in harmony with the universe,' and certainly, it is a lot more than the placement of objects or furniture.

I hope that I've been able to provide an idea of how much of a rich and diverse science Feng Shui is and that you are able to gain some insight into how it has evolved and developed over the years. At the same time, I hope that you are also able to contextualise Feng Shui as part of the wider field of Chinese Metaphysics and see that the real world of Feng Shui is about so much more than what people perceive Feng Shui to be.

又再笑談風水

Is It Science or a Sign of Superstition?

The Yi Jing is known generally as the Book of Changes, 易經
and claimed to be the oldest of the Chinese classic texts. It
describes an ancient system of cosmology and philosophy
which is known to be the heart of all Chinese science,
culture and way of life. The philosophy centers on the
ideas of the dynamic balance of opposites, the evolution
of events as a process, and the acceptance of the inevitability of
change. However, to many in Western cultures, the Yi Jing is
seen only as a system of divination.

The Yi Jing is one of the five classics in the Confucian cannon.
It is a collection of texts of philosophy and divination based
on a set of 64 hexagrams comprising various combinations of

又再笑談風水

broken and unbroken lines reflecting the relationship between the two basic forces of the universe, nature and human society – yin and yang.

Unfortunately, this well-known classical Chinese text has been used to derive a variety of modern day superstitions and a lot of "Feng Shui symbology." I want to explain a little the extent to which Feng Shui, be it Classical or New Age Feng Shui, draws on the Yi Jing and also to explain the role in which the placement of objects and symbols plays in Feng Shui.

First things first – it's not the I-Ching. This is a frequently used but incorrectly written term appearing in Western books that Romanized Chinese words using the old Wade-Giles format that dictates it should be spelt as I-Ching. However, it should be spelt Yi Jing. It may sound trivial but I feel it is important to start off correctly by pronouncing and spelling it properly.

Origins of the Yi Jing

The Yi Jing originally started out as a philosophy. It began in the Shang Dynasty (1600 – 1045 BCE) and was intended to be a sort of manual on life, a guide on how to conduct one's self morally and ethically, and how to effectively rule a country. This was especially prominent  during the times of Confucius where the Yi Jing formed the majority of his teachings. This was many thousands of years ago and you do need to maintain that perspective when thinking about the Yi Jing.

又再笑談風水

Later, during the time of King Wen (Zhou Dynasty: 1045-221 BCE), the Yi Jing was given a fresh perspective – some of its principles were transformed into a divination science. Hence, the famous "Ten Wings of Yi" were born. It was also during this time that the method of divination known as Zhou Ji came to be and was made part of the Yi Jing.

Yi means "change" and Jing means "classics" or "sutra."

To effectively accomplish this – at a time when education was privilege – the original images and symbols of the Yi Jing were removed and only the concept and mathematical aspects were maintained, and used to extract information about times, space, probabilities and events.

The original Yi Jing is a book on Philosophy. Yi means "change" and Jing means "classics" or "sutra." When the concept from Yi Jing was later borrowed to develop the divination science of King Wen, it came to be known as Yi Gua. Today, the Yi Gua method is known as Jin Qian Gua (Turtle Shell + Coins Divination Method).

Yi Jing and Feng Shui

Many Feng Shui practitioners like to say Feng Shui is "derived" from the Yi Jing – this statement is not entirely correct. You see, if you trace it far back enough, almost every type of Chinese study from the Chinese Five Arts (Mountain, Medical, Divination, Destiny and Physiognomy) has some connection to or roots in the Yi Jing.

山醫卜命相

The science of Feng Shui is derived from the concept of Yi but it is not based entirely on the Yi Jing principle simply because the Yi Jing is a philosophical book of a divination science. Feng Shui is neither. Schools of Feng Shui such as Xuan Kong Da Gua 玄空大卦, Xuan Kong Fei Xing 玄空飛星, Ba Zhai 八宅, San Yuan 三元 and San He 三合 have principles founded on key elements of mathematical science like that of yin and yang, the five elements and the hexagrams and triagrams. But these are derived from the concept of Yi and not verbatim translation from the Yi Jing texts themselves.

The concept of Feng Shui is all about Qi in our environment – how to derive and harness it to benefit us by making use of our property to tap onto this Qi.

This is the key goal of Feng Shui. We should not forget this. Whereas the Yi Jing texts today are either primarily a philosophy (the Tao) or a divination science, it does not directly address Feng Shui concerns.

Yi Jing Imagery vs Feng Shui Science

Many of the modern-day New Age Feng Shui ideas are supposedly derived from the image of the Ba Gua (eight trigrams). What has happened is that its imagery that was once used as a "teaching aid" or aide-de-memoir has been converted into the Real McCoy.

Images of the Ba Gua of the Yi Jing are supposed to be used to help students or Feng Shui practitioners appreciate how Qi works in a visual way. So for example, the hexagram Qian is represented as Dragon Flying into the Sky. The idea is to help people appreciate that Qian Gua refers to Qi that rises upward and/or a type of Qi that is very strong "like" a dragon flying into the sky. Along the way, this simple teaching aid has been corrupted into symbology and superstition.

Now, as much as we would like to believe that a figurine of a Dragon Flying in the Sky means Qian Gua, what you have in your back garden is just a teaching aid. It has no energy of any kind and it certainly does not bring about the Qi associated with Qian Gua to that part of your home.

Images or symbols in the Yi Jing are metaphors used to describe a scenario. They are not to be taken literally. Of course, this is not to say there is entirely no symbology in Feng Shui. The hulu 葫蘆 (or Calabash – a type of fruit) is a good example of this. The hulu (the natural kind, not the 32-karat gold or plastic kind) symbolizes Dui Gua 兌卦 because of its natural shape and its opening. Dui Gua in Feng Shui terminology is the number 7. It is for this reason that the hulu is said to have the natural ability to help ward away illness, which is the number 2 – in Feng Shui He Tu Numerology, 7 and 2 combine.

However, the hulu that was mentioned in Xuan Ji Fu texts refers to the hulu Shan (a mountain that is shaped naturally like a hulu). Thus, the ancient philosophers clearly understood that the need for symbolism only refers to "natural" objects – like mountains, rivers or a type of fruit. It was never meant to be that a man-made "symbolic" object should serve the same purpose as surely, with the superb craftsmanship in the old days, these symbols would have been easy to make and replicate. Then why isn't this mentioned in any of the ancient Feng Shui texts?

If we check it out closely, the symbols in the Yi Jing are limited to 64 items with subtle variations. But if you take a look around these days, so many Chinese symbols not even remotely associated with the Yi Jing are passed off as Feng Shui. So I am not sure how these symbols that have supposedly been "derived" from the Yi Jing came to be.

The hanging of calligraphy for instance – such as the word Fu (prosperity) that's supposed to be hung upside-down, or the Chinese word Xi (double happiness 雙囍臨門) used during weddings - is now misunderstood and passed off as Feng Shui. These Chinese characters or symbols were meant to set the mood for the occasion – a prosperous wish for the Lunar New Year or blessings of joy for the newlyweds. They were certainly not meant to and do not generate Qi and neither is this written down anywhere in the Yi Jing .

The concept of Feng Shui is all about Qi in our environment – how to derive and harness it to benefit us by making use of our property to tap into this Qi.

The truth about object placement

Understandably, it can be quite difficult for many people to know when an object is simply symbolic or decorative, and when it has true Feng Shui usage. This is because even in Classical Feng Shui, practitioners "place" items in the home. It is not uncommon for Feng Shui practitioners to ask clients to place aquariums or wind chimes in certain sectors.

The key is to always understand the origins of Feng Shui usage and its underlying purpose. Many of the items that have become associated with symbolism in Feng Shui application – these have simply become corrupted along the way. For example, the fixation with "Fishes" as bringing Wealth Qi originates from the use of aquariums in Classical Feng Shui. You see, water helps collect Qi in Feng Shui so modern-day practitioners, recognizing that a bucket would look ugly in a house, asked clients to set up an aquarium.

If you really have to use objects in Feng Shui, here's a simple guide: Ask yourself – what is it "made of" and not what does it "symbolize." The material, physical substance does have some small elemental value that can help influence the Qi in an area – for instance, an aquarium (water element) or wind chimes (metal element). If you have to consider the symbolic value, check if it is the creation of nature – like mountains, landforms, rivers and large rocks.

Natural symbols have Qi but don't get carried away. A little common sense goes a long way. So the next time you hear something that sounds a little outrageous ask yourself, "Is it science or a sign of superstition?"

又再笑談風水

Objects and the Ever-Popular 'Put Theory'

One of the most popular questions I get asked in emails as well as at public events is this: "Joey - what do you PUT in your office?" Of course, the answer that I don't 'put' anything in my office is a bit of a surprise to them. How can I not have anything in my office for wealth enhancement, or health improvement or to ward off the 5 Yellow Star?

Indeed, visitors to my office are often surprised by my unlikely collection of 'Feng Shui charms and cures' - they include a piece of abstract art (which I have absolutely no idea what it means!), Spiderman figures, a Collector's Edition Darth Vader figurine and collectible figures from my favourite Japanese anime, Naruto. And no, before you go out and buy some on eBay, these are not Qi-collecting or Sha Qi-defusing objects. I have them because I like them and I get some amusement from looking at them in my office.

Clients are often perturbed when I have no specific recommendations on colours or objects to be placed in certain places and items to ward off negative Qi. But the truth is, the practice of classical Feng Shui entails very little 'putting,' shall we say. A classical Feng Shui practitioner will rarely ask you put something in your room or wear a certain something. Indeed, if they ask you to do this and promptly open up their car boot to reveal their 'Feng Shui' wares in six different colours (one to match your sofa!) or usher you into a storeroom with ornaments of every size and incarnation, you should be a little suspicious.

Real Classical Feng Shui is Invisible Feng Shui

I do not advocate 'putting objects' as part of Feng Shui for several reasons. Firstly, classical Feng Shui, when practiced at its highest level, is completely subtle and nuanced. If you, the average layperson, enter a building and you KNOW it's been Feng Shui-ed, then the Feng Shui practitioner has probably failed at his or her job. The purpose of Feng Shui is to enable natural energies in the environment to be tapped for beneficial, productive use by the residents of the building or the area. It is not to turn your home into a Chinese restaurant and it certainly does not involve strange interior decoration ideas.

In classical Feng Shui practice, the goal is to make use of the good areas and reduce the usage of the negative areas, while ensuring there is good Qi collection and distribution. Those of you who are somewhat familiar with my talks and writings will know that this does not necessarily require a mountain-load of doohickeys and objects.

The essence of classical Feng Shui practice in the 21st century involves understanding modern life and then integrating Feng Shui into it. For example, in the old days, a piece of art or a fine vase or an antique object would draw people into a room in someone's house. The Feng Shui practitioner would advice the house owner to place this object in a certain room so that more people would enter and mingle about in the room. Now, the Feng Shui practitioner's objective was to encourage greater usage of the room, and to achieve that he used something subtle like the beautiful vase, knowing that if he told the house owner to just 'use the room more' he would get a blank look. Unfortunately, people then mistakenly assumed that it was the vase which was supplying the Feng Shui, instead of the room.

| Paintings | Good Fortune Vase | Auspicious Carpet Motifs |

| Bar | Living Room | Entertainment Room |

In modern times, to encourage greater use of certain rooms, Feng Shui practitioners might suggest that a client use the room for television-viewing, or perhaps as a living room or entertainment area.

Secondly, if you are to utilise Feng Shui for a business advantage, obviously, you do not want too many people to know you have this advantage, correct? Now, logically, when your office screams 'Feng Shui,' not only will other parties know that the business or person is using Feng Shui, but technically, they would also be able to 'defeat' or nullify that Feng Shui advantage. You can just imagine it now, the Feng Shui Wars - business rivals nullifying or countering each other's Feng Shui with their own cures, or going into a business negotiation and getting an upper advantage by wearing a cure that 'defeats' the other side's Feng Shui. If this boggles the mind, and sounds downright ludicrous, it is! That is why object-based Feng Shui does not really make sense.

Put Theory Breeds Paranoia

Another reason why I am not a proponent of the Put Theory is because it encourages people to be paranoid, and to place an inordinate amount of faith in an object. Classical Feng Shui does not involve being afraid or worshipping an object. It is about the natural energies in the environment, pure and simple.

Check the ancient classics if you have doubts, as none of these books prescribe the need to use an artifact to ward off bad Qi or to generate wealth out of thin air. Many ancient classics like *Qing Nang Jing* 青囊經 *(Green Satchel), Di Li Bian Zheng* 地理辨正 *(Discerning Truth of Earth Principles)* and 入地眼 *Ru Di Yan (Entering Earth Eye)* are reproduced in their original texts by many Hong Kong and Taiwanese researchers. You can find them in many Chinese bookstores. These books document the practice and study of Feng Shui since the Tang Dynasty. Read them and you'll discover that these books don't mention anything about the Put Theory.

When people objectify Feng Shui, they become ruled by the object that they believe encapsulates their good luck or bad luck, as it were. This encourages superstition and a closed mind. A person can't move out of a house because, oh, it's been good for 20 years, so let's not move, even if the new place is better from a classical Feng Shui standpoint. Similarly, by letting an object be the basis for a person's success, it encourages people to believe that the stairway to riches lies in the right object, and not with good old-fashioned hard work. No need to work hard, or think about whether you are doing the right thing or are in the right line. Just place [insert favourite wealth-making object] in your personal Wealth or Lucky corner and watch the money grow.

There is no 'one object that rules them all' when it comes to classical Feng Shui. Tapping into Qi can be done through a variety of subtle means, depending on what technique the Feng Shui practitioner wants to employ, and what options are indicated in the area and environment, as well as in the forms. Sometimes it involves the placement of Water in certain locations, but more often than not it is about avoiding the use of areas with strong Sha Qi or that are afflicted by Sha Qi and using the areas with positive Qi instead.

Sometimes, a problem is not related to Feng Shui but simply the luck cycle the person is in, based on his or her Destiny Chart. If that is the case, then an object is even more unlikely to be able to help the person. Think about it: how can pendants with a dragon or a rooster on it help prevent a problem that is caused by the shifts in energy, brought upon by the planetary movements? Are we saying that a mere pendant can change the course of the planetary influence or alter the magnetic pull of the planets on the Earth? Obviously not. Nothing is going to shift the energies, but your own actions can help reduce the impact of whatever influence the energies are creating. For example, if as a result of the elemental energies of the Bing Xu 丙戌 (Fire Dog) year, you are having problems with your boss, then you need to either moderate your behaviour towards your superior, or keep a low profile this year to avoid making the situation worse. Wearing a pendant or keeping a rooster on your table is not going to work unless these objects remind you to mind your manners with your boss!

What about the Hulu and Wind Chime?

In select and rare instances, specific items that have a clear elemental connection are sometimes used by some classical Feng Shui practitioners to resolve certain problems. One form of cure that actually has a proper basis in classical Feng Shui is the use of the hulu, commonly known as the Calabash in English. It is a real fruit (a Gourd, to be exact) and was originally used by Chinese herbalists as a container for medicine. Being a fruit that exists in nature, it is regarded as having natural Qi and so is sometimes used by Feng Shui practitioners. The fruit itself has two sections and has an opening on top. The dual-sections represent Heaven and Earth while the opening on top means that it belongs to the Trigram Dui 兌.

In the study of classical Feng Shui, Dui Gua or Dui Trigram belongs to the element of Metal and is also the #7 star. Typically you hear people using the calabash to help with illness but most people don't know why. #2 is the sickness or illness star, and in He Tu numerology, #7 and #2 combine. Hence, this explains the use of the Hulu to defuse the negative Qi of the #2 star. However, this technique can only be utilised when an actual, real, grown-by-Mother-Nature gourd is used, and not a resin or plastic version! While this is generally not my preferred technique, I am not opposed to its use.

Another acceptable 'object' that is typically used in some classical Feng Shui practice is the wind chime. It is used to introduce the element of Metal into an area. Again, this is fine as long as it is a wind chime that is actually made from Metal. However, if you find you don't like the

又再笑談風水

noise, you can actually use anything metal – pewter ware or your old sports trophies for example. I know some practitioner friends who insist on using real 24-carat gold items to utilise the real effects of Metal Qi! I personally would prefer not to resort to the use of elemental cures and try to keep things as 'natural' as possible. If the Qi flow is already good, oftentimes you'll find that no cure or object is needed.

All classical Feng Shui practitioners have their own style and pet methods. There is nothing wrong with using a Hulu or wind chime, as long as it's clear why it is being used and it relates to the true elemental nature of the item and not just to the imaginary aspects of 'put theory!'

Metal Qi

又再笑談風水

To Title or Not to Title

As Feng Shui is something that's close to my heart, I'm often reflecting on the state of the Feng Shui profession here in Malaysia. In this piece I want to share some thoughts I have on the conditions of its progress and development locally. It's a topic that is ripe for plenty of observation – both good and bad!

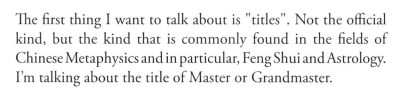

A Master by Any Other Name

Of late, it seems, there seems to be a clear lack of ethics, integrity and professionalism in the Feng Shui industry. It's sad to see such practices perpetuated by those who claim to be classical Feng Shui practitioners when these are the very practitioners who should be striving to improve the image of Feng Shui.

The first thing I want to talk about is "titles". Not the official kind, but the kind that is commonly found in the fields of Chinese Metaphysics and in particular, Feng Shui and Astrology. I'm talking about the title of Master or Grandmaster.

There is a huge fixation in this profession with the title Master or Grandmaster and it is not just an Asian thing. Even my Western students want to know when they will be accorded the title 'Master' and when I will 'grant' them this title. I always tell them, you can call yourself 'Master' when you think you're ready to be a Master.

The fact of the matter is that the title is hugely impressive to clients and students but really, it's not a testament to anything. This is because unlike the title of Master or Grandmaster in chess, which is awarded by a sanctioned world chess body FIDE, the title of Master or Grandmaster when it comes to Feng Shui is not awarded by any centralised body or international body. Basically, you can call yourself Master if you want and who is to question you on your right to do so? Heck - call yourself Grandmaster or Great Grandmaster. How is anyone to challenge your right to call yourself that?

Hence, the term 'Master' and 'Grandmaster' can be hugely misleading and lead people to assume that the person is highly skilled or experienced. This is especially the case when the titles are self-awarded.

Personally, I don't use the title 'Master.' I do have clients who call me Master but I try my best to dispense with that kind of title. I ask my clients to call me Joey or if they prefer to keep things formal, Mr. Yap will suit just as well. I prefer to refer to myself as their Consultant or I say I manage their Feng Shui and BaZi needs and concerns. You could say I prefer to take my cues from the industry's approach in Hong Kong.

In Hong Kong, the cradle of Feng Shui, Feng Shui practitioners don't call themselves Master. There simply is no equivalent Cantonese or Mandarin word for that term. Most of my masters in Hong Kong (and I'm using the word 'masters' here in the context of schoolmaster or academic master) ask me to call them Sifu or Lao Shi or even 'Ah Sir' (sir in Cantonese).

Of course, there are some true long-dead famous figures in Feng Shui, who have been posthumously called Grandmaster by the Feng Shui community as a whole. Yang Yun Song 楊筠松, author of the *Green Satchel Classics, Han Long Jin* 撼龍經 and *Yi Long Jing* 疑龍經 is often referred to by today's students of Feng Shui as a Grandmaster simply because his books are considered the classical texts and groundbreaking works on Feng Shui.

In this business, it is important to maintain a healthy sense of reality and have one's feet firmly planted on the ground. If you are an expert, you don't need to have a title to affirm that. How you speak to people will tell people you are someone with substance and skill and your results will speak for themselves.

Walking the Talk

The Feng Shui profession in Malaysia has come a long way of late. But it seems there is much more to do before those in the profession can move closer towards 'walking the talk.' We've come to a stage when marketing Feng Shui, and approaching Feng Shui as a business practice, is quite acceptable to the lay public. People now understand that Feng Shui practitioners are merely consultants for hire, like specialists and consultants in any other field.

In that light, it is important to ensure that as practitioners, a strong sense of integrity, ethics, and professionalism is maintained.

In that light, it is important to ensure that as practitioners, a strong sense of integrity, ethics, and professionalism is maintained. There's nothing wrong with taking a traditional approach but combining it with a professional approach – providing written reports, letting the clients know what they can reasonably expect from the consultation (rather than making wild statements about striking the lottery), ensuring that we provide a high quality of service to clients - will do much more to improve the image of Feng Shui than any title can ever achieve.

Claims like being able to change a person's life overnight, especially with regards to their bank balance, is definitely not what one might call ethical.

It is time that the Feng Shui profession moves away from this mentality as a whole. Money, of course, is important and wealth solves a lot of problems in this lifetime, but it also makes people hugely susceptible to hiring a Feng Shui practitioner purely on the basis of which Feng Shui Master claims to be able to make the client richer. Although it is easy to get business by telling people you can make them billionaires, claims such as this overlook the fact that in the end, the real results created are a result of the clients' hard work and entrepreneurial spirit.

Remember that Feng Shui can only help you achieve your endeavours. It certainly won't drop a bag of money on your doorstep and you will still need to work hard to achieve your goals. Any practitioner telling you different really needs a conscience-check.

As a simple rule of thumb, when faced with such a claim, consider things logically. If it really was so easy to make millions, wouldn't your Feng Shui practitioner be laughing all the way to the bank in a Rolls Royce? You don't have to doubt Feng Shui, but you should have a healthy curiosity about the practitioner you're about to engage and any extravagant claims he or she makes.

Most of my Feng Shui studies was done in Hong Kong and having studied with a number of Masters there, I admire the level of professionalism and integrity among the practitioners in a country where Feng Shui is employed extensively.

It is my sincere hope that the same level of ethics starts to seep into the local profession of Feng Shui consulting.

> *You don't have to doubt Feng Shui, but you should have a healthy curiosity about the practitioner you're about to engage and any extravagant claims he or she makes.*

又再笑談風水

又再笑談風水

The Myth Behind Lineage

A booming demand for Classical Feng Shui services and knowledge all over the world is making the business of Feng Shui more competitive. Naturally, some of the most intense competition is being felt in Hong Kong and Taiwan, the main source of much of today's knowledge in classical Feng Shui.

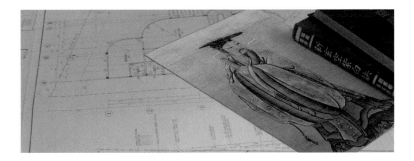

又再笑談風水

In the past, subtle marketing tactics were used, but this has changed more recently. In attempting to draw and attract clients or pupils these days, the latest tactic used by some practitioners is to play the lineage card. For as much success as the respective practitioners may have had with this approach, it has led to even more confusion for the new user of Classical Feng Shui.

In fact, I get lots of questions on this very subject. Considering the hype surrounding it, many of you may rightly wonder, "What is the significance of 'lineage' and what bearing does it have on picking a qualified Feng Shui practitioner?"

The Lineage Tree :

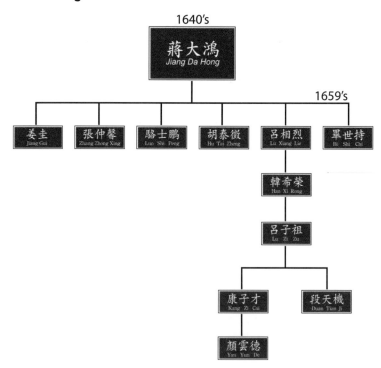

The Stuff of Kung Fu Movies

The concept of lineage has been popularized not so much by Feng Shui Masters but by Chinese Kung Fu movies. Those of you who are fans of these movies will know how the story usually progresses. It's a familiar scene: the dying Master usually summons forth his most loyal pupil or perhaps his most talented pupil and in a shabby hut, mossy cave or dark dank valley, hands over a blue covered book or withered scroll containing 'the great secret' of techniques or teachings. After a few muttered cryptic lines that are key to deciphering 'the great secret,' the old Master dies.

Of course, if you notice, all of these movies are set about 400 years in the past, when being a student meant that you actually were a disciple who would follow your Sifu around for half your life, doing lots of chores for him with the hope of being taught the great techniques and practices on the job. Today, the concept of 'indoor disciples' is rare. Feng Shui education, like any other form of education, is about paying fees and attending lectures! It has become a free-market practice. And

those blue-covered books containing 'the great secret' are freely available at the corner Chinese bookstore. As for the cryptic lines that are the key to deciphering 'the great secret,' most reputable Masters who teach and practice are quite happy to 'reveal all' to paying students.

Secret Manuscript

Feng Shui Genealogy

Naturally, Feng Shui also has its own lineages – this is true. Some lineages are extensive and can be traced back quite accurately. So, it is always more impressive to belong to a reputable Feng Shui lineage – at least this is perceived to add credibility to the master's knowledge and skills. However, fast forward to today's modern world and you will find that the term lineage has been used a little too loosely and flagrantly. It is an open secret that Feng Shui lineage can be easily created and that simply no one will suspect or question the origins of a lineage if a practitioner claims he has decades of experience by virtue of his age. Intentionally or unintentionally, the significance of lineage has been overblown when in fact lineage is the weakest consideration in the selection of a Feng Shui teacher or a Feng Shui service provider.

And just like some of the more exciting Kung Fu movies, you will hear of some of these Feng Shui practitioners claiming to be the sole lineage holder in possession of the 'secret' scripts passed down from their Masters, who conveniently handed it to them just before they breathed their last. It's all very stirring and enthralling, but sadly, not very substantial or meaningful.

What constitutes a Lineage?

又再笑談風水

If they are really of a particular lineage, they should be able to trace their roots of knowledge back to the original Ming or Qing Dynasty. That is what is known as a lineage. Simply being able to name one or two teachers you studied with is not what is traditionally referred to as a reputable and an authentic Feng Shui lineage. And furthermore, if you are a lineage holder, which ancient Feng Shui classics are you referring to? For example, student of the Wu Chang school of Feng Shui would have references to the original classical texts written by Great Grand Master Shen Zhu Reng 沉竹仍 and the founder of the lineage, Zhang Zhung Shan 章仲山.

Some Feng Shui practitioners today even claim their decades of experience constitute a lineage. This is not accurate, a proper system of lineage goes back hundreds of years and not only do the lineage carriers document all their cases, they also make it a point to document what works and what doesn't in practicing their system. In the present environment where anyone with gray hair can claim to be a lineage holder, it's important to verify their claims. If gray hair was a testament to grand lineage, then all the residents of the local old folks homes might very well be lineage holders as well.

If they are really of a particular lineage, they should be able to trace their roots of knowledge back to the original Ming or Qing Dynasty.

又再笑談風水

Attending a class or a course with a Feng Shui school is not equivalent to being a lineage holder either. In today's environment of study and teaching, it is more likely that you paid a fair course fee to undertake  a Feng Shui course with a Feng Shui practitioner or Master. Like any university or college you may have attended, you are a student of that school. You do not gain a lineage by attending a particular class; you merely receive certification or accreditation for having taken the course. A clear distinction needs to be made between the lineage concept and that of studying with a particular school or Feng Shui Master, otherwise, the lines become blurred and the layperson is easily misled by all this talk of inherited knowledge.

Another Marketing Tool?

Lineage today is partly a romanticized concept, but mostly, it's a marketing tool that is often used a bit too loosely to gain some commercial advantage. Though it may be reassuring to know that a Feng Shui practitioner is from a certain reputable lineage, the number of authentic lineages in the study of classical Feng Shui is actually quite few. The layperson may not always be aware of this, so don't always take it at face value when a Feng Shui practitioner claims to be of a certain lineage – ask him or her, politely and respectfully, about the roots of his or her lineage. Who are their teachers? Who taught their teachers? Do they have the exact lineage tree?

Does Lineage Translate to Superior Knowledge?

又再笑談風水

Assuming that your Feng Shui consultant or your Master is an authentic lineage holder – are they better than or more superior to consultants who are not lineage holders? Well, the answer is NO, not necessarily so. Much depends on the individual himself – whether he himself is good enough to make the most out of the knowledge offered by his lineage. To put it more precisely, lineage can only be taken as one of the positive reference points for a Master but certainly not a deciding factor for your decision to hire the services of that Feng Shui Master. The decisive factor is whether or not the Feng Shui skills of the Master are genuine, whether his Feng Shui knowledge is sound, authentic (traceable to classical texts), practical, useful, effective and beneficial to the clients. The significance of lineage should therefore not be over-exaggerated. Lineage means nothing if the practitioner himself is not good enough.

The decisive factor is whether or not the Feng Shui skills of the Master are genuine, whether his Feng Shui knowledge is sound, authentic (traceable to classical texts), practical, useful, effective and beneficial to the clients.

Clan Mentality – A Barrier to Knowledge

Obsession with lineage can also be a barrier to knowledge or an obstacle to learning. Their devotion and single-minded focus on only the texts of that one particular lineage can sometimes lead to a dogmatic approach and ignorance of the effective techniques and theories of other schools of Feng Shui. For example, in the old days, there was much debate over whether the San He school of Feng Shui was more effective or the San Yuan school of Feng Shui produced more measurable results. This resulted in both schools missing the obvious point – why not apply the theories from each other's school and achieve even more exceptional results? Devotion to lineage and fixation with the supremacy of their own theories lead to a lack of development in looking for methods to combine the theories effectively.

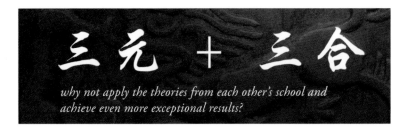

why not apply the theories from each other's school and achieve even more exceptional results?

In today's learning environment, a lineage approach can prove to be a limitation in truly gaining effective knowledge of Feng Shui. Yes, it may be reassuring to learn from an authentic lineage holder in the sense that it is a testament to the quality of the knowledge you receive. From a consulting point of view, however, it can be limiting and restrictive. If in today's world, computer programmers cannot simply learn one programming language, why should the expectations of Feng Shui practitioners be any different? In today's world, the more effective practitioners and teachers in Hong Kong and Taiwan are those who have studied multiple schools or systems of Feng Shui, BaZi and other fields of Chinese Metaphysics. A professional practitioner is one who can integrate different systems, different schools and different practices into his work without conflict.

It goes without saying that expectations of loyalty to a certain lineage are a thing of the past. Today, students who learn Feng Shui are fee-paying students. They are not beholden to the Master or the school for anything. Again, let us look at a modern educational context. A person can be a proponent of Keynesian economics, but does that mean they forsake all other economic theories? How can there be growth and development in any science if the dogmatic approach is maintained? Indeed, how can we know if one theory or approach is more superior to another, if we know nothing about the opposing theory?

So we come back to the question: does this lineage stuff matter? Does the pedigree of your Feng Shui master matter? After all, Deng Xiao Peng once said, it doesn't matter if the cat is black or white, as long as it catches mice.

It doesn't matter if the cat is black or white,
as long as it catches mice.

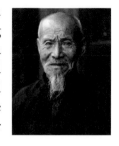

First, if you intend to pay for pedigree, then you should make sure that you are getting a pedigree. Researching and establishing a master's pedigree is important if you intend to learn and study from the person based on his or her claim of lineage, or if you are paying premium to this person purely for this claim.

Having said that, the concept of lineage may not be applicable in today's teaching and learning atmosphere. Study all that the various schools of Feng Shui have to offer and apply that which is relevant to a particular situation – should an individual school not have a technique to cope with a unique Feng Shui requirement, look to the other schools that may have a workable solution. That is what I try and emphasize to my students in the courses that I teach all over the world.

If you are hiring a consultant, you might consider asking questions on lineage, but perhaps it is more relevant to ascertain what systems of Feng Shui he or she practices and how well he or she knows those systems. In practice, Feng Shui consultants cannot afford to be pigeon-holed by lineage either. Feng Shui Consultants provide a service – we troubleshoot for clients, solve their problems and help them achieve their goals. To rely on one method alone to achieve this aim is simply not practical or feasible any more. A good practitioner is one who can integrate different systems, different schools and different practices into his work without conflict.

Tread Not On the Dark Side

Mountains are one essential part of the Feng Shui equation. The other equally-important part is Water.

Water is the Yang aspect of the environment because Water is always moving; hence, it is regarded as Yang. As I have always emphasized, an ideal Feng Shui environment must always have Yin and Yang in balance. So if you have Mountain, you must also have Water. Likewise, if you have Water, you must also have Mountain. Remember, the goal in Feng Shui is always balance.

Mountains are one essential part of the Feng Shui equation. The other equally-important part is Water.

又再笑談風水

Despite the importance of this simple basic principle of Yin and Yang in balance and the importance of having both Mountain and Water, many people unfortunately are not aware of this Feng Shui fundamental, or they're unaware of its significance. They only remember the second half of the saying, "Water governs Wealth" and forget the first part, "Mountains Govern People." This has not only led to an unhealthy fixation with Water when it comes to the Feng Shui of property, but also a tendency to resort to artificial means to get the Water.

Now, the first thing to realise about Feng Shui is (and I know I am going to disappoint a lot of people with this statement): you can't fake it. You cannot make it, and by extension it follows that you cannot fake it. It has to be naturally-occurring; present in the environment, naturally, be it the Water, or the Mountain. Now, you can 'improve' what is present in the environment to a certain degree, but this is more applicable to large-scale developments where they can undertake mass-scale landscaping, rather than to residential properties. But even a property developer cannot 'make' a mountain, or create a true river.

The reason why I want to emphasise this point about Water is because many people have unwittingly trod down the path of 'the Dark Side,' lured solely by the promise of great and immense wealth. What is this 'Dark Side,' you might ask? It goes by the name of 'Water Dragon.'

又再笑談風水

Separating Real Dragon from the 'Lizards'

What is this Water Dragon you might ask? It is supposedly a 'secret' formula from an old book called *Di Li Wu Jue* 地理五訣 (*Earthly Principles, Five Verses*) that states that if Water enters at a certain direction, and exits at another direction, then the property will create great wealth and immense riches for the occupants. There are countless classes and courses out there which offer these 'secret' Water Dragon Formulas, often at exorbitant prices. Unfortunately, this is really a case of paying for a Dragon, but getting a lizard. Why is that?

Firstly, many people are not aware that this formula is actually not really a secret formula but one that is freely available in most Chinese bookstores. So this 'secret Water Dragon' is really nothing special.

Secondly, this book is actually a compilation of environmental factors based on the alternative principles of San He, written during the Qing Dynasty. It has to be used very carefully, with all the chapters read in its entirety without looking at any of the formulas in isolation. Furthermore, the formulas have to be qualified by the presence of certain environmental features, as is clearly stated in the text.

Thirdly, taking a formula from the text and assuming it is gospel is always dangerous because it is not just about the formula, but knowing in what circumstances it can (or cannot) be used.

又再笑談風水

As I always emphasise to my students - the formula in itself is worth nothing if there is no understanding of how it is to be used, when it should be used, and more importantly, when it should not be used. If you're paying for knowledge, then you would rather pay for the understanding and not just the formula. If you just want a formula, buy the book. If you are interested in the Water Dragon formulas, I have reproduced some here. It pays to understand the strengths and weaknesses of the formula because it comes with certain side effects. After all, you do not take drugs without knowing what is going to happen to you, right?

A formula is like a recipe - anybody can get a recipe, but a skilled cook is what makes the difference between the cake coming out like in the picture in the cookbook, and a tasteless product unfit for consumption. The moral of the story? Feng Shui is not about paying for a formula. A true Feng Shui consultation is personalised for the individual - so if all you are getting is a standard formula (or a list of formulas), then you are not using effective Feng Shui because it is not personalised for you.

A true Feng Shui consultation is personalised for the individual - so if all you are getting is a standard formula (or a list of formulas), then you are not using effective Feng Shui because it is not personalised for you.

Drains for Wealth or Draining Wealth?

The most recent incarnation of the 'Water Dragon Formula' that I have seen and heard of involves drains and koi ponds. I have had clients who asked me to align the pumps in their koi ponds to follow the secret Water Dragon formula by having the pump pouring water into the koi pond at a certain direction, and a second pump that drains water at another direction. I have also seen clients who, in their desire to achieve a Water Dragon in their property, dig a drain around their property so that water enters and exits at certain directions.

Now, this is not at all what the text envisaged. How can a drain make you rich? If that's the case, everyone in Malaysia should be rich because all houses have drains here. And they don't call it a 'drain' for nothing! Also, the formation of water in the manner of a drain running directly across the Main Door ends up creating Sha Qi such as Cutting Feet Water, rather than ushering in positive Qi.

A DRAIN FOR WEALTH? A drain supposedly representing a Water-Dragon exit point in the garden of a house.

Special Water Dragon Exits From Di Li Wu Jue 地理五訣

Door Direction		Best Exit		2nd Grade		3rd Grade	
S1 丙 Bing	S2 午 Wu	W3 辛 Xin 285°-300°	NW1 戌 Xu 300°-315°	S3 丁 Ding 195°-210°	SW1 未 Wei 210°-225°	E1 甲 Jia 75°-90°	
S3 丁 Ding	SW1 未 Wei	SE2 巽 Xun 135°-150°	SE3 巳 Si 150°-165°	SW2 坤 Kun 225°-240°		–	
SW2 坤 Kun	SW3 申 Shen	E3 乙 Yi 105°-120°	SE1 辰 Chen 120°-135°	S3 丁 Ding 195°-210°	SW1 未 Wei 210°-225°	W1 庚 Geng 255°-270°	
W1 庚 Geng	W2 酉 You	N3 癸 Gui 15°-30°	NE1 丑 Chou 30°-45°	W3 辛 Xin 285°-300°	NW1 戌 Xu 300°-315°	S1 丙 Bing 165°-180°	
W3 辛 Xin	NW1 戌 Xu	SW2 坤 Kun 225°-240°	SW3 申 Shen 240°-255°	NW2 乾 Qian 315°-330°	NW3 亥 Hai 330°-345°	–	
NW2 乾 Qian	NW2 亥 Hai	S3 丁 Ding 195°-210°	SW1 未 Wei 210°-225°	W3 辛 Xin 285°-300°	NW1 戌 Xu 300°-315°	N1 壬 Ren 345°-360°	N2 子 Zi 360°-15°
N1 壬 Ren	N2 子 Zi	E3 乙 Yi 105°-120°	SE1 辰 Chen 120°-135°	N3 癸 Gui 15°-30°	NE1 丑 Chou 30°-45°	W1 庚 Geng 255°-270°	
N3 癸 Gui	NE1 丑 Chou	NW2 乾 Qian 315°-330°	NW3 亥 Hai 330°-345°	NE2 艮 Gen 45°-60°	NE3 寅 Yin 60°-75°	–	
NE2 艮 Gen	NE3 寅 Yin	W3 辛 Xin 285°-300°	NW1 戌 Xu 300°-315°	N3 癸 Gui 15°-30°	NE1 丑 Chou 30°-45°	E1 甲 Jia 75°-90°	E2 卯 Mao 90°-105°
E1 甲 Jia	E2 卯 Mao	S3 丁 Ding 195°-210°	SW1 未 Wei 210°-225°	E3 乙 Yi 105°-120°	SE1 辰 Chen 120°-135°	N1 壬 Ren 345°-360°	
E3 乙 Yi	SE1 辰 Chen	NE2 艮 Gen 45°-60°	NE3 寅 Yin 60°-75°	SE2 巽 Xun 135°-150°	SE3 巳 Si 150°-165°	–	
SE2 巽 Xun	SE3 巳 Si	N3 癸 Gui 15°-30°	NE1 丑 Chou 30°-45°	E3 乙 Yi 105°-120°	SE1 辰 Chen 120°-135°	S1 丙 Bing 165°-180°	S2 午 Wu 180°-195°

□ Left to Right

▥ Right to Left

* Degrees are based on the Heaven Plate (Water Ring) of the San He Luo Pan

Di Li Wu Jue contains only a few of the many Water Formulas found in Classical Feng Shui. True application of Water involves the availability of mountain formations because mountain formations generate the Qi and Water harnesses the Qi. One is Yin, the other is Yang. You cannot have one without the other. When it comes to making use of a Water Dragon formula, one must use the right Water Formation based on the existing Mountain formation, and then select an appropriate door or house facing.

Unfortunately today, the approach is to build the Water based on the existing door of the house. The formulas have been diluted and bastardised to apply to drains and koi ponds, and have been modified to the extent that the environmental formation is ignored, and only the Main Door or facing is used to determine what the Water Dragon should be. This is incorrect.

Dragons, in the language and terminology of Feng Shui, refer to Water and it is Water that brings vibrant Qi, according to the old saying. So it is not wrong that Water indeed governs Wealth aspects. But, the classics, when they refer to 'Dragon', are referring to natural water, - creeks, rivers, lakes and ponds - that are naturally-present in the environment.

It is for this reason that you cannot 'make' a Water Dragon in your house. And indeed, you should not because you may find you make the situation worse, and not better. But the most important thing to remember about Dragons is that you must have them in conjunction with Mountains. One Yin, One Yang is needed in order to achieve balance. So do not be fixated with just Water and ignore the Mountain altogether.

To Consult or Not To Consult

Over the course of my career as Feng Shui consultant and teacher, I've been asked many questions related to the subject of Feng Shui in particular, and Chinese Metaphysics in general. Some of the questions are serious and merit some thought, some are rather amusing and merit a laugh, but all are asked in absolute heartfelt sincerity. One of the more common threads in the line of questions is a variation of the "How do I know what to expect from a Feng Shui consultation?" or "How do I know if the consultant is for real?" question.

又再笑談風水

This, I thought, would make an excellent topic to write about at length. What exactly is involved in a Feng Shui consultation? Do you need one? How do you get one? And what can you, as the person on the receiving end of the service, reasonably expect?

In Search of the Real McCoy

Perhaps one of the most troubling dilemmas is: how do we know that the person we just hired to inspect the Feng Shui of our property is for real? The answer is simple. You would approach it the same way you would look for a reliable doctor. You perform a check on their qualifications.

You ask for their background, their qualifications (on the subject of Feng Shui; such as what system of Feng Shui they apply), and their level of experience, affiliation and references. Do it just like you would when looking for any other service provider. There are many consultants around these days, so shop around. Talk with and ask for references from people who have had consults done.

Yin House Feng Shui

Tell the consultant why you are looking for a consultation; check to see if he is confident about handling your particular case. Sometimes, an inexperienced Feng Shui consultant may not be able to handle a very complex case. And they will tell you if that's the case. For instance, some Feng Shui consultants are experts in auditing Yin Houses (graveyards), but they can't do houses. Or they might be experts in handling landed houses but aren't so good at handling condominiums or apartments. (Didn't you know that there are 'specialists' in the practice of Feng Shui too?)

One the other hand, if you don't really have a problem, if things are going really well in your life – you DON'T need a consultation. Undertake a Feng Shui consultation because there is an aspect of your life you would like to improve, and not just because you want to 'keep up with the Joneses.'

又再笑談風水

Spotting a Quack

If he steps out of his car looking like a character from an episode of The X-Files, you need to be wary. Most Feng Shui consultants go to work dressed in the very same way you would dress for work – in professional office attire. He definitely does not strut out in flowing robes like he might have just come from a Jedi Council meeting, wielding a stick of incense instead of a Light Saber.

The next giveaway is usually his advice to 'enhance' or 'activate' every sector of your home with some specific item. Conveniently enough, he will have most of these items right in the trunk of his car, or as Yoda might say, "A large suitcase he may bring along!"

You might find yourself being the recipient of such bad news as, "Your house is infested with bad Qi" or worse, 'haunted,' and that you will need to pay a princely sum to have it all fixed. And bad things happen to people who don't get this 'infestation' taken care of, he might warn you. This is a typical scare tactic con artists deploy, so beware and be on-guard.

Another typical type is the one who will tell you that he has 'created' billionaires and that it is your 'good fortune' to have met him on that day. This always fascinates me – if a Feng Shui Master can create billionaires, why on earth is he still slogging away doing Feng Shui consultations for you and the rest of the world? Why doesn't he just make himself a billionaire? But perhaps I am more surprised by the fact that not many people challenge this type of claim made by the so-called Feng Shui practitioners.

What's In a Feng Shui Consult?

又再笑談風水

A proper Feng Shui Consult will often first involve the inspection of your external environment prior to taking a look at the internal layout of your home. If you're wondering why, it's because Qi originates from your external environment, and is NOT manifested inside your home or from any of the objects or corners inside.

Your consultant needs to verify the origins of this Qi before he is able to determine how he will harness it to benefit your home.

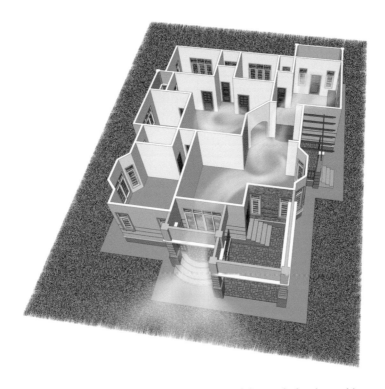

Your consultant needs to verify the origins of this Qi before he is able to determine how he will harness it to benefit your home.

For the interior, he would usually use the Eight Mansions, Xuan Kong Flying Stars or Xuan Kong Da Gua systems of Feng Shui. (There are other branches of classical Feng Shui systems too; you can ask him what he practices.) You would have seen him calculating or working with an energy map of your home after taking the relevant measurements and directions – this is also known as the Natal Charts of your home and may look to you like a tic-tac-toe grid with numbers in each of the boxes. Sometimes the calculations may look pretty complicated, involving several trigrams from the Yi Jing (Da Gua) method of assessment.

If he comes right in, walks around, and starts telling you about colors and décor – congratulations, you've just hired yourself an Interior Decorator. Not a Feng Shui consultant.

A genuine Feng Shui consultant will also ask for the date and time of birth for residents living in the house, or if it's an office, the birth data of key personnel. This is used to calculate a BaZi or Destiny Chart. This is how a Feng Shui practitioner DIAGNOSES his patients (residents of the property) before making out his prescription (Feng Shui remedies). If you don't see his analysis of your BaZi, ask him what method he is using to diagnose your problems – chances are you might not be getting the right prescription.

What Should You Prepare?

I do understand that many people fear bringing in a Feng Shui consultant because they might be told they need to undertake massive renovations or are forced to buy things that they don't need. A proper Feng Shui consultation does not always involve renovations; there are usually many alternatives that can be explored. It all depends on the skill level of your Feng Shui practitioner.

Classical Feng Shui remedies are usually very subtle. For example, it could be something as simple as changing your sleeping direction, rooms, or positioning of water features, or realigning your working desk. If you are unable to adjust your house's interior arrangement due to certain constraints, a good consultant will even be able to tell you what measures you can physically or mentally undertake to cope with the effects of your Feng Shui. What I mean by this is that certain 'actions' can be undertaken to fix a problem that might be evident in the present or sometime in the near future due to the Qi of the house.

A thorough consultation should always be done in various stages. You meet up with the consultant to discuss your scope of work, and he will then come to your property to inspect it, after which a summary of the consultation is prepared and you would have a follow-up meeting with him to be briefed on the findings. It should take about two to three weeks for the complete consultation, unless there is a real urgent need on your part.

又再笑談風水

Could a consultation be done in two hours? Of course, but expect a real rush-job with no proper report and a mainly verbal rundown on what needs to be done. Don't be surprised if you forget what your consultant told you during the consultation. This is the reason why Feng Shui consultants today prepare proper reports and maintain documentation. You can even engage your consultant to work hand-in-hand with your interior designer or architect, saving you the hassle of being the go-between and running the risk of miscommunication.

I hope this has helped answer some of your questions and concerns regarding engaging a Feng Shui consultant, and provided you with a thorough enough guideline on Feng Shui consultations to set your mind at ease.

Who's Best Directions?

I had just landed at Kuala Lumpur International Airport, strolling out of the arrival lounge in my usual glad-to-be-home fashion when I caught a man intently peering at me.

I don't consider myself a particularly good looking person, so I politely smiled at him. He took this as an invitation to speak.

"Are you Joey Yap?" he asked me.

I was trying to think if somehow I owed him money as I answered with a cautious, "Yes, good to meet you."

又再笑談風水

"I am Mr. Chow. I sent you a question and you have yet to answer me," he said, sounding very much like I owed him money.

It turned out he was a big follower of my TV show and also the weekly columns in the New Straits Times. I explained to Mr. Chow that as much as I would like to answer the questions sent to me, my mailbox has been piling up and I may not be able to answer all of them.

That would have been the end of the discussion if he had not grabbed my hand and said, "I NEED you to answer just this ONE question. My marriage depends on it."

Now, when someone says that, you can hardly just walk away. In the interest of his family's happiness, I asked him what I could do to help.

"My wife is an East Group and I am a West Group Gua, we were told we need to sleep in separate rooms! What should I do? My wife has threatened to stop cooking if I go ahead with this Feng Shui technique. And if you know my wife, you would know she is not a woman to be trifled with," he lamented.

So, what REALLY is the Eight Mansions System of Feng Shui?

This is not an uncommon question I get and I did take some time to address this in my TV program, but Mr. Chow most likely missed that episode!

For those of you who are new to classical Feng Shui, the Eight Mansions is one of various systems of classical Feng Shui. And many of you may have already heard of the 'your best personal direction' concept. Basically it categorizes people into East Group and West Group – each with positive and negative directions based on the 8 cardinal directions of the compass (North, Northeast, East, Southeast, South, Southwest and so forth).

And many of you may have been told that East group people must make use of the East, South, North and Southeast as their good sectors/directions; while for West Group people, the West, Northwest, Northeast and Southwest holds true. You can refer to the table below for a clearer picture:

East Group 東命

Gua 卦	生氣 Sheng Qi	天醫 Tian Yi	延年 Yan Nian	伏位 Fu Wei	禍害 Huo Hai	五鬼 Wu Gui	六煞 Liu Sha	絕命 Jue Ming
Kan 坎 1 Water	東南 South East	東 East	南 South	北 North	西 West	東北 North East	西北 North West	西南 South West
Zhen 震 3 Wood	南 South	北 North	東南 South East	東 East	西南 South West	西北 North West	東北 North East	西 West
Xun 巽 4 Wood	北 North	南 South	東 East	東南 South East	西北 North West	西南 South West	西 West	東北 North East
Li 離 9 Fire	東 East	東南 South East	北 North	南 South	東北 North East	西 West	西南 South West	西北 North West

West Group 西命

Gua 卦	生氣 Sheng Qi	天醫 Tian Yi	延年 Yan Nian	伏位 Fu Wei	禍害 Huo Hai	五鬼 Wu Gui	六煞 Liu Sha	絕命 Jue Ming
Kun 坤 2 Earth	東北 North East	西 West	西北 North West	西南 South West	東 East	東南 South East	南 South	北 North
Qian 乾 6 Metal	西 West	東北 North East	西南 South West	西北 North West	東南 South East	東 East	北 North	南 South
Dui 兌 7 Metal	西北 North West	西南 South West	東北 North East	西 West	北 North	南 South	東南 South East	東 East
Gen 艮 8 Earth	西南 South West	西北 North West	西 West	東北 North East	南 South	北 North	東 East	東南 South East

Just as a person has a Life Gua, the House also has a distinctive Qi map and is classified as one of the 8 types of Guas.

Now, it is inevitable that at some point, a wife will discover she and her husband are not of the same Grouping or vice versa. And then the debate about sleeping in different beds, facing different directions, or studying in different parts of the house becomes an issue. I have even heard of couples who sleep in the same bed, but with their feet facing each other, in order to achieve their best personal directions. Should a Feng Shui system really divide a happy couple in such a fashion?

If it sounds like hogwash, you are right. It is.

This whole situation stems from a lack of authentic education on classical Feng Shui and also a lack of proper literature on the Eight Mansions system of Feng Shui. The truth is: the Eight Mansions system of Feng Shui has another important piece of information that is often less discussed - the House Gua. Just as a person has a Life Gua, the House also has a distinctive Qi map and is classified as one of the 8 types of Guas.

This knowledge is actually clearly written in the original Eight Mansions Feng Shui classics: *Eight Mansions Bright Mirror Classics* and *Golden Star Classics*.

The 'Secret' of the House Gua

You simply cannot practice Eight
Mansions Feng Shui without knowing
the House Gua. It would be like trying
to play tennis without a tennis racket!
This piece of information is so crucial
as to be considered the missing link in
your practice of Eight Mansions Feng
Shui. There is a huge relationship
between your personal Life Gua (think
of it as your personal energy map) and
House Gua (house energy map).

Many people make this mistake of buying or renovating
their house based solely on their personal Life Gua (or Ming
Gua). This can often cause friction between a husband and
wife; in today's world where both the husband and wife
work, who is to be regarded as the breadwinner and whose
Gua then takes precedence?

How can two people get along like this when one person's best
direction is the other person's worst? And which East is the
best? Will facing East in Bangsar or Kepong or Subang Jaya
deliver the same results? Of course it won't!

Why? Because you will be living in a different house that
has its own HOUSE Gua and each House Gua has a
different Qi map that alters or determines the quality of
your individual Gua.

This is why, as the ancient classics clearly taught us, there is the need to consider the quality of Qi in the house and to make doubly-sure they even labeled it EIGHT MANSIONS system of Feng Shui in reference to 8  different types of House Gua. Somehow along the way, this crucial piece of information was lost and everyone came to know only about the personal Life Gua, leading to many an unhappy wife or husband who felt they had to 'sacrifice' for their partners' wellbeing.

Some students are even unclear on some of the terminology used in the Eight Mansions system of Feng Shui. They refer to a person's third best direction as Nien Yien when it should correctly be referred to as "Yan Nian". I am not sure how this came to be or who propagated this but the translation must have been lost when it was translated into English. Ironically, when you pronounce the words incorrectly like this – it means something else altogether.

In fact, the 8 House Gua and the 8 Life Gua work hand-in-hand as the two key pieces of information required when applying the Eight Mansions system of Feng Shui.

Good for Both Parties

Even if a loving couple belongs to 'different Life Gua groups,' all you need to do is identify which sectors of the house are suitable for BOTH of them based on what's good in the house. A house has its own good and bad sectors too. Thus, regardless of whether you belong to the East or West group, all you need to do is to identify which are the good sectors of the house and use them accordingly. Then, your problem is fixed!

As you progress further in your study of Eight Mansions Feng Shui, you will learn more advanced methods like Xing Gong Sheng Ke 星宮生剋 (Star versus Palace Growth and Counter Relationship) and the 8 Wandering Stars of Eight Mansions method 八遊星 (Ba You Xing), all of which are advanced systems of Eight Mansions Feng Shui.

So the next time you come across someone looking to split up you and your partner, remember, it is not called the Eight LIFE Gua system of Feng Shui, it is rightly called the Eight MANSIONS system of Feng Shui.

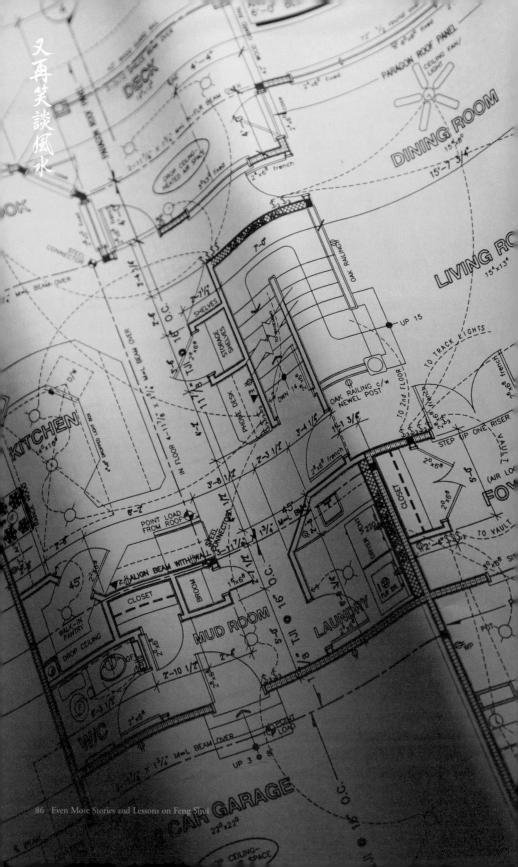

又再笑談風水

又再笑談風水

Simple ways to get started in Feng Shui

I am going to tell you about the time I was in Canada to conduct some courses on Feng Shui and BaZi. During the lunch and coffee breaks, there were lots of opportunities for all of us to chat  and get to know each other. I was intrigued by the fact that so many students told me how surprised they were that Feng Shui was so straightforward – it seems many of them had in the past found their study or attempts to practice Feng Shui complicated by an uncertainty over a very simple yet fundamental question: when you Feng Shui a house, what do you focus on first?

Yes, this seemingly simple and elementary question is in fact what boggles many people when it comes to Feng Shui. Perhaps it is the result of information overdose but many people often have no idea where to start when it comes to practising Feng Shui, especially if they are planning to 'Feng Shui-It-Yourself' their home or office. They wonder about the ornaments on their dressing room table, ponder over the colour of their curtains, sweat over the plants in their garden, and worry about the furniture they bought last week.

So it seems like I should devote some attention to this at length: if you want to Feng Shui your house yourself, what should you be looking into when it comes to checking or improving the Feng Shui of your home? I'll also show you a simple, easy and very quick DIY Feng Shui technique in this chapter.

Think Environment, Forms and Qi

The fact is that when it comes to Feng Shui, it is simply not possible to overstate the importance of the external macro environment. Now, that has nothing to do with economics but plenty to do with the formation of mountains and rivers in the vicinity of your home or property. A good Classical Feng Shui practitioner will always look at these natural features, known as Landform (巒頭 Luan Tou) or Forms, before he or she evaluates the Feng Shui of the property. These Forms are what dictate the quality and type of Qi that influences the area and of course, your property.

A good Classical Feng Shui practitioner will always look at these natural features, known as Landform (Luan Tou) or Forms, before he or she evaluates the Feng Shui of the property.

In addition to the Forms, which determine if there is positive or negative Qi in the area or if the Qi flow is somehow being blocked or repelled, formulas must always be considered. Formulas, which are techniques and calculations for determining the energy map of an area or a property, help to qualify the Forms, assess the quality of Qi and provide a fuller picture of the Feng Shui situation in the area.

Finally, when it comes to the property itself, classical Feng Shui practitioners will always zero in on the three most important factors: the **Main Door,** the **Kitchen** and the **Bedroom**. In fact, when it comes to evaluating the property itself without looking at the macro environment and the formulas, these are the three areas that should always be given priority. These three important factors are known as "Yang Zhai San Yao."

You might be wondering why is it that only the Main Door, the Kitchen and the Bedroom are considered important? As I have said in the past, Feng Shui is a very practical, logical and rational practice that has no room for frivolity. The Main Door is given significant priority because this is the entrance to the house, for the residents of the property and for the Qi. The Main Door is considered the Qi Mouth of a home. Accordingly, it is extremely important to make sure that you have a good Main Door as this will go some way towards ensuring you have good Qi entering the property. The Main Door is considered the primary reference point in any system of Classical Feng Shui.

又再笑談風水

Ensure suitable locations for bedroom and kitchen

The Kitchen is where food is prepared and so is also extremely important. Food is what nourishes us and gives us energy and strength to go about our endeavours. Hence, the Kitchen should be located in a suitable sector so as to ensure the vibrant health of the residents. Finally, the bedroom is where we spend time resting and sleeping. Out of 24 hours a day most people spend between 6-8 hours in their bedroom. Accordingly, it is important that the bedroom is located in a place that is conducive for rest, recovery and sleep with stable and rejuvenating Qi.

If you can look at nothing else, make sure that the above three factors are well taken care of and you would have taken some important positive steps towards improving the Feng Shui of your property.

Applying Simple Feng Shui to Your Home

For the average person, evaluating the external macro environment and Landforms is not something they can do or for that matter, should be expected to be able to do without some expert help. So if you want to Feng Shui-It-Yourself, what then can you do? Well, the easiest and quickest form of evaluation that the average person can do when it comes to the Feng Shui of their home is to look at the house itself in tandem with a simple formula-based assessment of the three important factors: the Main Door, the Kitchen and the Bedroom.

The technique that I am going to show you how to use is known as the Life Gua Method, which is derived from a system of Feng Shui known as Eight Mansions or Ba Zhai. It is premised on the theory that every individual is imprinted with certain energies at the time of his or her birth, based on the planetary influences and magnetic fields exerting an effect on the Earth. These energies are unlocked or maximised best when used in tandem with certain directions. A simple analogy would be to see the Life Gua as your personal radio frequency and the directions as the antenna that enables you to 'tune into' that frequency.

I have selected the Life Gua Method because firstly, it is a safe method with minimal negative side effects, even if applied incorrectly. Secondly, it is quite an easy method to use and usually brings about a modest improvement.

The three important factors: Main Door, Bedroom, Kitchen.

Thirdly, it is a system of Feng Shui that produces very steady improvements, and thus is suitable for people residing long-term in a property.

So how do you make use of the Life Gua Method? Begin with your year of birth. Check the Gua Table below and find your Life Gua number. Do note that the number differs depending on your gender. Once you have found your Gua number, match it to either the East Group or the West Group directions table below. From here, you can derive your personal Favourable and Unfavourable Directions.

East Group 東命

Gua 卦	生氣 Sheng Qi	天醫 Tian Yi	延年 Yan Nian	伏位 Fu Wei	禍害 Huo Hai	五鬼 Wu Gui	六煞 Liu Sha	絕命 Jue Ming
Kan 坎 1 Water	東南 South East	東 East	南 South	北 North	西 West	東北 North East	西北 North West	西南 South West
Zhen 震 3 Wood	南 South	北 North	東南 South East	東 East	西南 South West	西北 North West	東北 North East	西 West
Xun 巽 4 Wood	北 North	南 South	東 East	東南 South East	西北 North West	西南 South West	西 West	東北 North East
Li 離 9 Fire	東 East	東南 South East	北 North	南 South	東北 North East	西 West	西南 South West	西北 North West

West Group 西命

Gua 卦	生氣 Sheng Qi	天醫 Tian Yi	延年 Yan Nian	伏位 Fu Wei	禍害 Huo Hai	五鬼 Wu Gui	六煞 Liu Sha	絕命 Jue Ming
Kun 坤 2 Earth	東北 North East	西 West	西北 North West	西南 South West	東 East	東南 South East	南 South	北 North
Qian 乾 6 Metal	西 West	東北 North East	西南 South West	西北 North West	東南 South East	東 East	北 North	南 South
Dui 兌 7 Metal	西北 North West	西南 South West	東北 North East	西 West	北 North	南 South	東南 South East	東 East
Gen 艮 8 Earth	西南 South West	西北 North West	西 West	東北 North East	南 South	北 North	東 East	東南 South East

Each of these directions is not just merely 'favourable' or 'unfavourable'. There are specific types of energies in each direction that are suitable for a specific use or function. For example, the Sheng Qi direction taps into Life Generating Qi, suitable for increasing work performance and vitality, while the Tian Yi direction taps into healing energy that is favourable for health or rejuvenation. The Yan Nian direction is all about communications and interpersonal relationships while the Fu Wei direction is best used for calming, peaceful and relaxing activities, such as meditation, personal cultivation or just to get a good night's sleep.

Let's take an example to give you an idea of how to make use of the Life Gua Method. For example, a female born in 1957 will have a Gua number of 8. She belongs to the West Group of Directions, thus her Favourable Directions are South West, North West, West and North East. Her personal Unfavourable Directions are South, North, East and South East.

How then do you apply this information to your property? One way is to check to see if your Main Door taps into any one of your Personal Favourable Directions. You can also make use of this system in the bedroom, by making sure that your bed headboard faces one of your Personal Favourable Directions.

Now, the Life Gua Method is not by any means the most powerful form of Feng Shui you can use, nor is it the only method of Feng Shui out there. It is also a method that has some qualifications and limitations, especially for properties with more than one resident. Suffice to say, this is a simple and easy technique for anyone to 'get their feet wet' with Feng Shui with minimal fuss. Plus, there are no expensive renovations required or cures to implement so do give it a go!

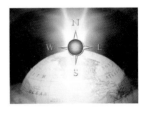

Now, the Life Gua Method is not by any means the most powerful form of Feng Shui you can use, nor is it the only method of Feng Shui out there.

又再笑談風水

Old Practice in a New Era

One of the challenges of modernising a profession like Feng Shui lies in changing the way Feng Shui is practiced. The public still has a persistent, old-fashioned idea of what a Feng Shui practitioner is like - that they should all turn up in Mao suits or Shanghainese long dress, speak in cryptic phrases and offer a few short words of advice, and then disappear from sight, never to be seen again. If you have a problem, don't call them, maybe they will call you. If things don't work out, well, that's to be blamed on your fate or destiny. If you want to know why certain suggestions are made, the answer is you don't need to know, just do it.

This is very much an outdated manner of practice, which functions very heavily on what we call 'Master-worship' (where the Master is held in such awe that he is not to be questioned), and that takes it for granted that the average layperson need not know why the master is doing something, they should simply trust him to do it and follow his advice. And this is not really how most Feng Shui practitioners work and practice anymore these days.

It's a modern world and like any other profession, Feng Shui practitioners have to move with the times. That means trying to bring a measure of professionalism to how they offer their services to the public and how they deal with the public. In this piece I'm going to delve into what you, the public, should expect when you deal with a Feng Shui professional in this day and age.

Improving Impressions

Understandably, many older masters in the profession still go about their practice in the old-style way. Certainly, we cannot expect sudden modernization out of a profession that has only really been openly practiced since the turn of the last century. This takes time. However, the trend is slowly and gradually changing - you can readily see this in Hong Kong, where more and more Feng Shui consultants now ply their trade from a proper office, and do so in suits and ties.

Of course, the newer generations of consultants are looking to take Feng Shui to an even more professional level. Feng Shui today is a service industry. It is striving to be on par with any other kind of consulting business, as Feng Shui consultants help clients determine what their problems are, and help them solve their problems. And so clients have a right to be treated like they would by any other service industry professional, be it a doctor, dentist or an accountant.

The new generation of Feng Shui consultants are professionals.

Improving House-side Manner

In the past, the Feng Shui master turns up at your doorstep, makes a few remarks, tells you what to do and then is off. Nowadays, clients demand a proper meeting and follow-up sessions, wherein the Feng Shui consultant ensures that the recommendations have been properly implemented. Part and parcel of taking Feng Shui to a professional level is changing the way this service industry has always been practiced. This includes providing written reports for clients so that they do not have to take notes on what they are supposed to do to improve their Feng Shui. Reports are often supplemented with photographs, so that the clients know exactly what they are supposed to do. To ensure that a complete service is provided to the clients, usually the Feng Shui consultant will also select a suitable date for ground-breaking or renovations to commence.

Professional consultants do not leave their clients in a lurch when something has gone wrong and certainly, no professional Feng Shui consultant will tell his clients that 'it is their fate' that the situation has become such. If the Feng Shui consultant has been thorough in his job, he would have studied the BaZi or Destiny chart of his clients before making any Feng Shui recommendations. If, for example, a client's destiny does not demonstrate a capacity for great wealth

or high status there is already an inherent limit to what the Feng Shui consultant can do. Contrary to what most people think, Feng Shui consultants cannot fix and solve all problems – they can only help their clients within capacities they are capable of possessing.

Contrary to what most people think, Feng Shui consultants cannot fix and solve all problems – they can only help their clients within capacities they are capable of possessing.

In this day and age, confidentiality is also something that many clients value and increasingly, it has become an important hallmark of Feng Shui consulting. You wouldn't want your accountant spilling the beans on your books, and similarly, you don't want your Feng Shui Master telling everyone in the world that your house and office and factory have all been Feng Shui'ed. Now, there is nothing wrong in seeking the services of Feng Shui professionals, but just like doctors, accountants or any other profession, client confidentiality is something that modern day Feng Shui professionals must respect. Imagine your Feng Shui Master going round attributing all your business success to his proclaimed Feng Shui skills, completely disregarding your own hard work and efforts!

The client, of course, is not bound by such a confidentiality requirement but the Feng Shui professional must always be the soul of discretion. This is especially the case when it comes to BaZi (Astrology) consultations, where the consultants are often privy to very sensitive or delicate situations and clients must feel free to speak about any matter without worrying that it will make the 6 o'clock news!

Professionalism in how Feng Shui practitioners behave and act is also something that the profession is looking to improve. Most practitioners do not want to be known as a bunch of curt, tight-lipped professionals who only offer up five words of cryptic advice, and then leave the clients to figure out what it is that they meant. Lest you think I'm joking, there used to be a very famous Feng Shui master, reputed to be the master who advised Mao Tse Tung, whose words of advice never went beyond five Chinese characters. He was nicknamed Bu Guo Wu and he was an extremely famous Master in China in the last century.

Today, going to a Feng Shui consultant is like seeing a doctor – you're entitled to understand what the problem is, how the diagnosis is reached, and the prescription for your problem. Getting the right 'house-side' manner is something I try to emphasise a lot to my students – we cannot afford to be so old-fashioned in our approach anymore. In any case, being open and willing to provide explanations to a client's questions is the best way to deal with a client's reservations or concerns. Quite understandably, no one is going to undertake the particular renovations prescribed by a Feng Shui consultant, or perhaps, even do something as simple as change the room that they are sleeping in, unless the reasons are compelling enough and not frivolous.

Commercialisation without Selling Out?

又再笑談風水

I believe the next level of challenge for the Feng Shui profession is how the practitioners can take their knowledge and services to the public without cheapening the profession or encouraging a 'short-cut' mentality.

Commercialization is a necessary facet of every service industry but like doctors and dentists, who find a way to balance their Hippocratic oath with the need to make a legitimate living, Feng Shui consultants are striving to provide a legitimate service while making it as accessible as possible. But that doesn't mean that they are obligated to help everyone.

Unfortunately, one of the prevailing problems facing modern Feng Shui practice is that it is very often all too easy to resort to 'product recommendation' in order to make it accessible. The founder of Revlon, Charles Revson, once remarked about the cosmetics industry: "In the factory we make cosmetics, in the drugstore we sell hope." I do not like to think that Feng Shui practice is in the business of, to paraphrase Revson, "selling hope in a figurine," but unfortunately, this seems to be part and parcel of what commercialization brings.

"selling hope in a figurine"

Some of the ways to provide a measure of accessibility and affordability is through books, articles in the media, and attempts to correct the situation through education. Knowledge, after all, is power. But here too there are challenges. As more and more sources of information and books on Feng Shui appear, there are more and more opportunities for the practice of Feng Shui to be invariably tempted to stray from authentic methods and fundamental approaches in order to resort to the quick-buck method of product recommendation.

又再笑談風水

Frankly, I personally think there's nothing wrong with products per se. If someone tells me they get a psychological lift out of wearing certain colours, or certain motifs of Dragons inspire them, or reading motivational calligraphy on their walls makes them aspire to achieve more in life, or oriental-designed clothing empowers them (I like Shanghai Tang too!), that's okay. Positive thinking is never to be knocked, and it doesn't matter how you arrived at that positive state of mind. But what I think is quite wrong is to encourage the belief that a resin figure of a cat above your cash register is going to bring in business, or wearing a Dragon pendant is going to ward off your bad luck, and curing a 5 Yellow Sha problem is simply a matter of popping a cure in every West corner of your house. If only Feng Shui were that easy.

The Feng Shui profession is approaching a new renaissance. As expectations grow along with more knowledge and awareness, it is reassuring for the public that the level of professionalism in the practice of Feng Shui is improving and more practitioners are adopting a service-oriented approach. I look forward to the Feng Shui profession taking a greater step forward, towards encouraging greater understanding and recognition, while making it more accessible to everyone.

The Complex Task of Urban Planning

Feng Shui has increasingly become a selling-point for property developers these days. From a marketing standpoint, it is easy to understand why property developers are paying more attention to Feng Shui issues - more and more buyers nowadays are placing greater emphasis on Feng Shui considerations.

又再笑談風水

As the public becomes more educated about Feng Shui, developers have to be better-prepared to answer difficult questions when buyers approach them. Prospective buyers want to know where entrances to the townships are, what direction the entire development faces, and what direction the individual houses  are facing. Some even bring their own Feng Shui consultants to survey the area. Well-read prospective buyers may even come asking about the landform features of the property.

In response to buyers' expectations, property developers are increasingly conscious about Feng Shui considerations and some have even taken the initiative to involve Feng Shui consultants in the process of planning and developing property projects from malls to theme parks to residences.

So what exactly does a Feng Shui consultant do when it comes to large-scale property development projects? And how do you know if the Feng Shui component of a development is the 'real thing,' or just another marketing spiel? I'm going to share with you exactly what it is Feng Shui professionals do when they work on a large-scale property development project. By understanding what goes on when it comes to the Feng Shui of a large-scale property project, you will be able to understand what role Feng Shui plays in urban development. You will then know the right questions to ask a developer, especially if a key point in their marketing strategy is the fact that it has good Feng Shui!

Bringing Qi into the Picture

又再笑談風水

Today, many property development projects have a strong urban or town planning component to them because developers have to pay attention not only to the individual homes and the recreational facilities, but also to do the structure and building of everything from the roads and playgrounds to the clubhouses and marinas!

Undertaking the Feng Shui for a housing project or integrated property development is quite a complex and long-term engagement for most Feng Shui consultants. They are often on-board even before the project gets off the ground – at the planning and land selection stage – and frequently, this involvement continues throughout the development of the project, from the construction on the ground, up to the sales and launch of the project.

Often, the first thing the Feng Shui consultant does when it comes to a large-scale property development is select the land. Now, as most property development companies have a land bank, a proper Feng Shui consultation will involve the survey of all these properties usually from the air via helicopter in order to gain an insight into the contours of the land, including the mountain formations, streams, creeks, and natural ponds. It is not difficult to see the Dragon (land contour or mountain ranges) and how it turns, moves and flows on the land from an aerial view. From there, the Feng Shui consultant will usually be able to determine which piece of land is most suited for the development that the developer has in mind. Not every piece of land is suitable for a commercial residential venture, and using the land for the right purposes is the first step towards ensuring a good start for the development.

As most property development companies have a land bank, a proper Feng Shui consultation will involve the survey of all these properties usually from the air via helicopter in order to gain an insight into the contours of the land, including the mountain formations, streams, creeks, and natural ponds.

At this stage, the Feng Shui consultant may also start the process of troubleshooting and problem-solving. For example, what to do with pylons or other threatening features located close to the land the developer has decided to buy or has already bought? Most residential house buyers will refuse to buy a house near electric pylons, even if they know nothing about Feng Shui. But if the pylons are located in an appropriate sector, this danger can be reduced and prospective buyers can feel assured by the knowledge that this kind of problem has been correctly or adequately dealt with by the developer, in line with Feng Shui principles.

For this reason, you should make sure that when a developer says the property has been Feng-Shui-ed, you must ascertain at which point the Feng Shui consultant was involved. If the consultant is only brought on board after the development has been built, then chances are any improvements are likely to be purely cosmetic in nature. One of the important questions to ask is whether the consultant has been involved in the process of the land selection.

One of the important questions to ask is whether the consultant has been involved in the process of the land selection.

又再笑談風水

Melding Aesthetics with Qi Principles

Once the land has been selected, the next step is to work on the designs for the buildings, be it houses, apartments, office blocks or office towers. Here, the Feng Shui consultant will look at the preliminary design by the architects, and look for ways to find a synergy between the artistic and creative vision of the architect and interior designer, and the Feng Shui principles that need to be applied.

Most Feng Shui consultants would work with the building and house designs or apartment layouts and suggest modifications to accommodate the Feng Shui needs of the structure. Now, these changes are often subtle and imperceptible to the untrained eye. For example, conventional wisdom states that residential properties should be square as that is the shape of the element of Earth. Earth stands for stability in the study of the Five Elements. However, very few people would want to live in a completely square house or apartment. So, obviously, the Feng Shui consultant has to see if a more aesthetic design can work based on the landform of the area. Odd shapes, be it for houses, apartments or buildings, are actually acceptable in Feng Shui if the large macro environment and the landforms support such a design. If you go to Hong Kong, there are plenty of buildings with features that seem to technically violate every Feng Shui rule (sharp corners, sharp angles, pillars in strange places) in order to achieve a measure of aesthetic value. The Burj Al Arab Hotel in Dubai, the Louvre Museum in Paris and the HSBC building in Hong Kong all have unusual structural designs to accommodate aesthetic interests but they do not all have bad Feng Shui.

The Louvre Museum in Paris   *The Burj Al Arab Hotel in Dubai*

For buyers, often it is difficult to tell to what extent the Feng Shui consultant's influence is on the design. Good Feng Shui consultants do not make their work obvious to the untrained eye – otherwise, it's not Feng Shui! Suffice to say that if part of the marketing plan touts the colours of the property as 'Feng Shui colours' or claims that every property comes with stone lions at the entrance, you should take the 'Feng Shui virtues' of the property with a pinch of salt.

From the Macro to the Micro Details

Aside from the design of the apartments, offices or houses, the Feng Shui consultant also looks into the layout and flow of the roads and the overall infrastructure in the development. This is because roads are virtual rivers, and are thus carriers of Qi. It is essential to ensure that the roads are not aligned with void lines (where Qi flow becomes discounted) and that there are angles in areas where it's acceptable to have sharp angles because it doesn't affect any of the properties in the development.

Aside from the design of the apartments, offices or houses, the Feng Shui consultant also looks into the layout and flow of the roads and the overall infrastructure in the development.

If the Feng Shui consultant has done his job well, then something as minor as a lamp post placement would also be looked into and planned so that no prospective buyer is landed with a house that has a lamp post squarely in front of the main door (a big no-no when it comes to residential Feng Shui). The Feng Shui consultant will also ensure that each phase of the property is built to face suitable directions. For example, this may be done to avoid circumstances where certain phases of houses face a direction that is unfavourable or difficult to benefit from, based on the landform of the area. Or to avoid houses being inadvertently located facing a void line.

Water placement is also very important in Feng Shui. These days, it is common for many property developments to include recreational areas or playgrounds with lakes, or man-made creeks, fountains and swimming pools. The Feng Shui consultant, taking into account the layout and design of the entire master plan, will make sure that the water is located in an area that benefits the residents overall as well as being suitable for the location of Water.

Finally, the Feng Shui consultant will also select suitable dates for the ground-breaking work to ensure that the project gets off to a smooth start and there are minimal disruptions during the construction period, select dates for the hanging of the Main Door on the units, and also, select dates for the launching of the project to ensure good sales!

Beyond Flying Stars and Eight Mansions

You might be wondering what techniques come into play when it comes to large-scale development projects. For industrial and large-scale projects like resorts, theme parks, vast commercial residential projects, or even town planning, Feng Shui consultants are not using simple systems like Flying Stars Feng Shui and Eight Mansions Feng Shui. It's just not feasible. A theme park or town may have more than one entrance and exit – how do you determine which is the facing? The Feng Shui consultant will use different techniques for large-scale projects because the considerations and concerns, and indeed the scale, is quite different from undertaking the Feng Shui of one house.

Also, for theme parks, towns and resorts, the demands are quite different. For homes and residences, the priority is the needs of the residents while for a theme park or resort, the developer may not only want to generate good revenues, but also to ensure lots of visitors.

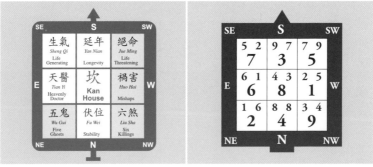

8 Mansion Chart   *Flying Star Chart*

So the next time you check out a property development project and are told that the 'Feng Shui' is good – make sure you understand the "hows" and "whys" of the property, and if the Feng Shui of the property is your paramount consideration, find out what are the 'Feng Shui features' that make the property so favourable. Positive Feng Shui is always a good thing to have when it comes to a prospective property investment but it's also important to make sure it's the 'real McCoy' and not just the marketing fluff.

The Road to Riches

If there are two things in this world that can make people try anything, it is money and love. Feng Shui, unfortunately, has been used as a means to sell people all kinds of items and trinkets in the name of helping them acquire more of one, and find the other.

I want to talk a little about what 'wealth' means in classical Feng Shui, and what is the rationale behind certain common practices that have become associated with 'wealth enhancement.' By understanding these basic fundamentals and appreciating the philosophy of Feng Shui, I hope that people will be able to then understand how to respond when they are faced with a 'Feng Shui' wealth-enhancing claim, or offered a magic 'Wealth' formula.

Think Vibrant Qi, not Wealth

又再笑談風水

The word 'Wealth' has sort of crept into the technical vocabulary of Feng Shui. Feng Shui practitioners use it as a catch-all term to explain the outcome of using certain energies or sectors in a property. Rather than getting all technical, they cut to the chase. Somewhere along the way, the concept of 'Wealth Sector' turned up. As I most likely have said before, Feng Shui doesn't actually speak directly of 'Wealth' or 'Money' in any of the classics. So a magical Feng Shui money-making formula is something that should definitely make you ask a barrage of questions rather than prompt you to reach for your wallet.

So what then do the classics like *Di Li Bian Zheng* 地理辨正 speak of? They speak of 'Prosperous Qi' (or Wang Qi 旺氣) and the means of identifying where Prosperous Qi resides. They speak of techniques and methods for gathering Qi and avoiding or transforming negative Sha Qi 煞氣.

The Book of Burial by Kuo Pu, one of the oldest classics on Feng Shui, explores the central tenets of Feng Shui that claim Qi gathers at the boundaries of water, and is dispersed by wind. It does not say: MONEY appears wherever there is an aquarium. It does not say: put eight goldfish into the aquarium and you will inherit a thousand/million bucks. It does not say anything about ships of gold in a room, paw-waving kitty cats above cash registers in stores and fountains in backyards.

Placing cat figurines on cash registers cannot generate wealth.

Getting the Vibrant Qi

Feng Shui is one of those practices in which complexity and simplicity are embedded within each other. You need to understand the basics to appreciate the complex formulas. But at the same time, memorizing formulas and being able to recite them by heart, without understanding the fundamentals of Feng Shui, are of no benefit either. That is why formula books are not the answer to successful Feng Shui application, because without an understanding of the fundamentals the formula is just a bunch of numbers. A cookie recipe doesn't make much sense to a person who doesn't know how to bake.

Feng Shui is one of those practices in which complexity and simplicity are embedded within each other.

When it comes to using Feng Shui to enhance Wealth opportunities, first we need to understand the type of Qi that can promote Wealth opportunities. In Feng Shui, we need to locate the 'Prosperous Qi.' To the average lay person, this is usually called 'Yang Qi.' However, Feng Shui practitioners refer to it by its more technical name, 'Prosperous Qi' or 'Wang Qi' (in Chinese) because Qi can be classified into 5 types of Qi according to its timeliness and at the professional level, it is important to know exactly what type of Qi and what stage of timeliness it is at.

又再笑談風水

I must dispel the notion that 'Prosperous Qi' can be somehow 'created.' You cannot 'create' Prosperous Qi by making an area more 'Yang,' by putting, say, red lights or bright lights in a certain area. The Qi has to have the Prosperous quality in the first place, based on the time period. Remember, in Feng Shui, we are interested in what is natural and prevailing in the environment, not what is artificial or man-made. In any case, you cannot simply decide that you want your Front Door to be where the Prosperous Qi is located and try to force the situation. The location of the Prosperous Qi is not dictated by convenience, but by the Qi map, as derived from the calculations. The name of the game is to work with what you have, without having to make costly and needless aesthetic changes to your house that make it obvious you are trying to 'Feng Shui' the place!

旺
Wang

氣
Qi

The location of the Prosperous Qi is determined through two methods: through calculations based on the direction of the property, such as Eight Mansions or Xuan Kong Flying Stars, and through evaluation of natural environmental features. Usually, calculation-based methods are used for Interior Feng Shui and the environmental features observation method, known as Forms, is used for External Feng Shui.

So for example, we want to locate the Prosperous Qi in a house that is facing the South 2 direction. The Prosperous Qi of the house is located where the Facing Star #8 position is, as you can see from the chart below. Each house of course will have its own Prosperous Qi location and the role of the practitioner is to locate this Prosperous Qi area.

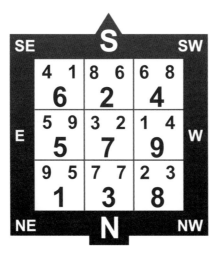

Period 7, Facing South 2

As the location of the Prosperous Qi is different based on the Qi map of the property and derived from the calculations, it is a fallacy to think that there is a standard universal 'Wealth Direction' for everyone. There isn't - it depends on your house direction. Now, you might notice that not everyone living on the same row as you (with houses facing the same direction!) is equally rich and wealthy. In the Feng Shui context, the external forms still have to be taken into consideration. But there is also the Destiny context - a person who lives in a house with a direction personalised to his/her Destiny will definitely have an edge over a person with a house that is less in-tune with his/her BaZi.

Once the location of the Prosperous Qi has been pinpointed, the Qi must be activated. Situating an activity room (such as the television room or living room) in this sector is one way of stimulating the Prosperous Qi in a location. Placing a Main Door in the Prosperous Qi location is also a form of activating Prosperous Qi in a suitable area. Sometimes, for the purposes of activating the Qi, Feng Shui consultants recommend that clients place Water in certain locations. It is purely to activate the Qi. It has absolutely nothing to do with the Water itself, or the fish in the water, but the Yang quality of the Water. Water, even when still, is always moving because the molecules continue to move. The fish just help to keep the Water active and also, provide some aesthetic benefit.

Water is placed in certain locations to activate the Qi in the area.

When you have the right type of Qi at hand, then you need to collect that Qi. There's no point in having the Wealth stars in the right location on the Flying Star chart, or locating the sector of Prosperous Qi, if the Qi cannot collect. This is where the landform of the environment, and the internal forms of the property, make all the difference. An extremely important aspect of Qi collection is having a good Bright Hall or Ming Tang as it is known in Chinese.

A Bright Hall is not a hallway with a lot of lights, nor is it a well-lit porch or an area in your house lit by a 100-bulb chandelier. If this is what a Bright Hall is, all the shops selling lights would be minting it! Instead, a Bright Hall is a broad, spacious and open area that enables Qi to settle and collect. Ideally, a property should have three Bright Halls, in tandem with the principle of Three Divide, Three Harmony (the San Fen San He formation).

Having it, making it and keeping it

又再笑談風水

Making more money and having more wealth opportunities is not just a case of fixing your Feng Shui. Your personal Destiny Code comes into the equation as well. Feng Shui cannot fix or give you what you in the first place do not have in your Destiny. So, you may need to re-align or moderate your goals, adjust your perspective, change your attitude, and see how Feng Shui can help you within the path that Destiny has laid out for you. Sometimes that means having realistic expectations. Sometimes, that means being prepared for hardship or being willing to take on certain challenges. Sometimes, that means adjusting the timing of your plans.

I might add that being rich does not mean that you have great wealth. It means you have the capacity to make money, and the means to hold on to it long enough to enjoy it. And even where people have the capacity and destiny for great wealth, it is not a guarantee that they will actually become rich, or fulfill their destiny.

Yes, you read it right. Some people actually do not fulfill their Destiny!

A Destiny chart may show a tremendous capacity for wealth or opportunity for wealth, but it will not become a reality if the person is unwilling to do what it takes to achieve his/her Destiny. BaZi tells you that you can be rich, but it does not always say: "It will come easy." There are no shortcuts in life!

Bill Gates

Why does Bill Gates still go to work every day? Has being the richest man in Asia stopped Li Ka Shing from continuing to pursue business opportunities? Destiny is but one part of the equation. Being willing to take the chance, make the sacrifice, face the challenges – those are the factors that make up the other component. Some people have a Destiny that demands hardship, great personal sacrifice, and even the experience of having gone through bankruptcy, divorce, bad relationships, and bitter family ties before they can see the pot of gold at the end of the proverbial rainbow.

Li Ka Sing

A Picture Guide to Feng Shui

People are often curious about how a Feng Shui audit is done, partly because by understanding how a professional consultant approaches his task, it is easier for the layperson to gauge the extent to which they can undertake the same task themselves. How else can you learn how to 'Feng Shui-It-Yourself' besides seeing how it is done by a professional? I always say to my students, do not be worried  about what you cannot do – focus on what you can. So keep that in mind as you read this. Using Feng Shui is about more than just hiring a Feng Shui master – it is about being committed to helping yourself and using Feng Shui as a means to that end.

又再笑談風水

Hence, in this I will share with you the 'trade secrets' on how Feng Shui consultants go about auditing and evaluating a property to determine if it is good, or not so good. To help you 'see' the Feng Shui, I have also included several pictures of the area.

Often people say they cannot see mountains (or Dragons) in their area. So, here is a picture of mountains taken in the vicinity of the house I audited recently. The first picture is a "Ju Men 巨門" Huge Door Mountain. The second mountain in the vicinity is a "Tan Lang 貪狼" Greedy Wolf Mountain. Now, I won't go into the specifics of where these forms ideally should be as there are complex formulas dealing with these issues. For now, focus on looking for an area or house, with mountains like these, which do not emit vicious Qi but are pleasant and noble-looking.

These are the facilitators of Qi in our natural environment. Preferably, the front mountain or "An Shan 案山" Table Mountain should not be too high - an easy way to find out is to stand at the Main Door, and extend your hand naturally. If the mountain is higher than your extended hand, it's too high. The mountain at the rear should have 3 'layers' - meaning, mountain ranges extending behind the nearest mountain, but if pressed, just make sure there is a higher mountain at the area or higher ground at least. Where these natural features are found, there would be circulation of positive Qi.

Huge Door Mountain 巨門山

Look for the Bright Hall

Generally, we want a nice big broad area in front of the house to act as a Ming Tang or Bright Hall to collect the Qi. The ideal is to have three layers of Bright Halls, so that one conforms to the "San Fen San He" Three Harmony Three Divide principle of Feng Shui.

Firstly, between the mountain range in front of the house and the house itself, there is a large Bright Hall, and then a smaller one inside the larger Bright Hall. So where's the third? It's in front of the house. Now, look at the house in the pictures below.

Generally, we want a nice big broad area in front of the house to act as a Ming Tang or Bright Hall to collect the Qi.

Notice that this house has a broad, wide and high space in the front? Now, when you have a nice broad Bright Hall in the macro environment, we want to 'mimic' this in the micro environment, as represented by the property itself. A house with a tight Bright Hall squeezes the Qi. Also, if the Main Door itself is a little high, this makes it hard for Qi to enter the property. However, this can easily be rectified and furthermore, the overall environment is still good. So the owner of such a house can benefit from the Qi, but perhaps will find it is a modicum harder, because he's not getting all of the Sheng Qi as a result of the tight entrance.

External Bright Hall

Find the Water - Look at the Roads

Now, the perfect environment in Feng Shui requires a mixture of both the Yin and the Yang. When mountains are present, the Yin element of the environment is already there. So, next we must look for Water or the Yang element. Remember, Qi gathers at the boundaries of Water. Roads act as carriers of Qi in the modern world that we live in. So, look at the roads in the area. A little bit of detail-consciousness is required, especially when the tilt of angle of the roads is very subtle. But if you look hard, you can see it.

Below is the picture of the road coming into a house 1. See how the road meanders down and is not a sudden steep incline? Then as it reaches the level of the house, it curves gently. Qi has gathered here. So all the owner has to do is tap the Qi, either by opening a door or adjusting the position of the house gate to tap the Qi.

The house in the picture also taps into the Qi brought down by the roads from higher ground. Again, notice that the roads meander down from higher ground and do not incline steeply. Qi likes to meander and move slowly and not gush down the road; otherwise, it becomes Sha Qi. Now, this house has the advantage of a broad Bright Hall, so the owner just has to open the main gate at the correct angle to tap the Qi.

又再笑談風水

又再笑談風水

The Feng Shui Way to a Better Wealth Qi

When we talk about wealth in Feng Shui, it's important to remember that it is not about money, lottery winnings, or windfall wealth. It is about opportunity and finding an environment in which to locate your home or office, one that lets you capitalise effectively on those opportunities to improve your wealth, achieve status or to simply live well.

Fei

Xing

Having said that, there are some simple basic techniques you can use to help improve your Wealth opportunities. I will introduce a system of Feng Shui known as Fei Xing or Flying Stars and show you how to use the Flying Star chart of your house or office to improve your Wealth opportunities.

Flying Stars is one of the most popular systems used by most Feng Shui consultants. Professionally, it is regarded as a fairly basic and simple technique, so it is suitable for use by most lay persons. Also, many people are quite well-informed these days about Feng Shui and so it is something that is quite manageable for most.

An important aspect of Flying Stars Feng Shui is the element of time. Time, in Flying Stars Feng Shui, is divided into cycles of Qi, with each cycle lasting 20 years. Under this system, no house or location is ever permanently good or bad. It changes with the passing of time and the shifting of Qi. The goal of the Flying Stars technique is to identify the most prosperous Wealth Qi or People Luck areas at a given point in time, bearing in mind the 20 year Qi cycle. It is a system for short-term and quick results, and is often used in Hong Kong and Taiwan.

Now, before we can delve into the Flying Star charts, I first need to talk a little about how to take a direction. The Facing Direction of your property is needed in order to plot the Flying Star chart of your property.

Finding the Facing

House Facing (Facade) + Door Facing

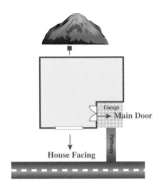

House Facing

Always use the façade of the house, or the direction the house has been built to face, to take the Facing Direction.

With a luo pan or Feng Shui compass (you can use a normal compass if you want but it requires you taking an additional step to identify the degrees according to the 24 Mountains), stand at the center of your property's facing direction. The facing direction is the direction in which the house is built to face or where the main façade is located. Do not just assume that your Main Door is the facing direction of your property. This is a common mistake that many people make. Always use the façade of the house, or the direction the house has been built to face, to take the Facing Direction.

Once you have a Facing Direction, you need to know if it is a Period 7 or Period 8 Flying Star chart. If you moved into your house between 2004 and 2023, then your property is considered a Period 8 house. If you moved into your house between 1984 and up to February 4 2004, then you have a Period 7 house. Now, based on the Facing Direction of your house and the Period of your house, find the Flying Star chart that matches your property, you now have the Qi map for your property.

又再笑談風水

Once you have established your property's Flying Star chart, transfer the Star numbers of the corresponding sectors onto a plan of your house. Follow the example below on how to transfer the Star numbers. This method will enable you to identify the part of the house in which the various Stars reside.

The third piece of information you need to have is to understand the difference between Facing Stars and Sitting Stars. The diagram below tells you which is the Facing Star and which is the Sitting Star on a Flying Star chart.

Facing Stars govern the wealth capacities of each sector whilst the Sitting Star governs the people or health capacity of the sector.

Three ways to improve your wealth opportunities

Once you have the Flying Star chart of your property or office, you need to find the Facing Star #8. Look at the example below. In this House, the Facing Star #8 is located in the Southwest.

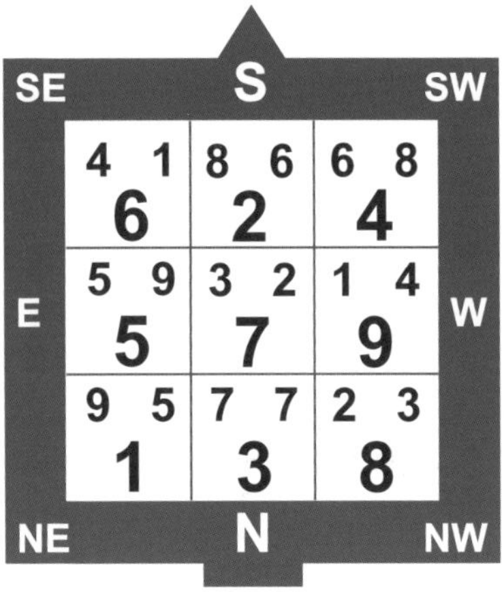

Now, let's say that for this property, there is a door located in this sector, as per the diagram below.

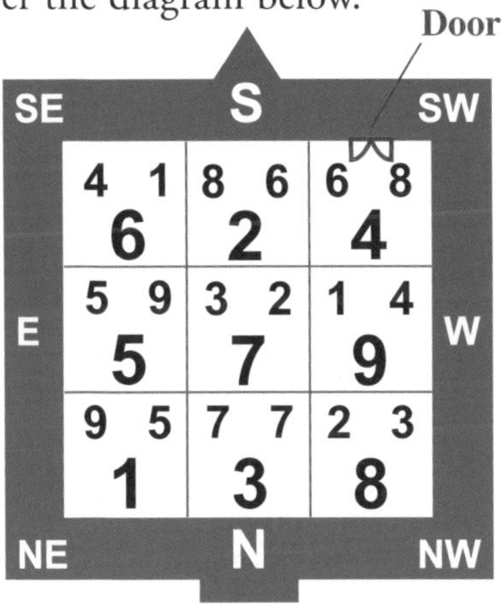

Door

Bedroom

Kitchen

In my practice and teaching, I have repeatedly stressed the importance of the 3 factors in Feng Shui. Make it your mantra: Main Door, Kitchen and Bedroom. As this property already has the Main Door located in the Wealth Qi location for Period 8, there's no need to enhance the house any further. Now, all we have to do is make sure that the surrounding environmental forms are supportive of this Main Door.

So, what if your property does not have a Main Door at the Facing Star #8 location? There are still a few tricks you can try. First, keep the area uncluttered and unobstructed, so that the Qi can flow and the Prosperous Qi the #8 star brings can move and circulate around the property.

In case you do not have a door at this sector, you can also try placing an aquarium or water feature outside the location of the Facing Star #8 or in a location that is convenient. In the study of Feng Shui, Water is a Yang form and is thus suitable for the stimulation of Qi at this location. As for how much water you will need, well, it depends on the size of the house or office. Obviously, if you have a large house, a goldfish bowl is not going to do you much good. However, if you have a small house, a 3-4 foot aquarium should be fine. Remember, use common sense and proportionality to guide your decision.

Here's a quick pointer on what kind of water features you can use, aside from an aquarium. Generally, I do not advocate the use of table fountains. This is because these types of water features usually contain, at most, only 3-4 small mineral water bottles' worth of water, which is usually not quite enough to stimulate the Qi.

Let's say for some reason, you cannot use the Facing Star #8. Perhaps it is located in a storeroom. Or in a location that does not permit the placement of Water. In that case, look for the Facing Star #9 and either place the Main Door there, or place a water feature or aquarium in that location. Using the Prosperous Qi of the next period, which is Period 9, will not bring immediate results but will enable you to lay the foundations for wealth in the future.

Thinking beyond the #8 Star

I often stress the importance of appreciating how BaZi and Feng Shui are inter-related disciplines that need to be used together to help a person achieve his/her full potential in life. Maybe some of you who are already quite well-versed in Feng Shui have activated the Facing Star #8 in your property, but are wondering why nothing seems to have happened. Typically, a professional Classical Feng Shui practitioner will always check a person's BaZi before making a Feng Shui prescription. Contrary to popular misconception, 'Enhance the #8' is not the only trick of the trade. It is just one of the very basic techniques in the armoury of the Feng Shui practitioner. But it is always important to establish the 'diagnosis' before we proceed with a 'prescription.'

Sometimes, the #8 star does not bring results because there is something standing in the way of wealth opportunities that the #8 star does not address. A person may be going through Rob Wealth (劫財 Jie Chai) luck, and so the problem is not that he/she is not making money, but that a joint-venture or partnership or perhaps even family members are draining him/her of financial resources.

It may be that the immediate environment around your property is not supportive of the #8 star, or is not conducive to Qi collection, so activating the #8 doesn't bring about significant results.

Look for the #8, but look beyond the #8 too. Forms, for example, play an important part in determining if the environment is supportive of your endeavours, or just barely helping you out. It may be that the immediate environment around your property is not supportive of the #8 star, or is not conducive to Qi collection, so activating the #8 doesn't bring about significant results. In the ancient classics, it is said, "There are no fake forms, and no real formulas". What is around you, and where you are located, must also be taken into consideration.

A Different Type of Seven Star

Sometime in 2007 I had been invited to the 2007 Wellbeing Show as one of the guest speakers. The Show was officiated by the UAE Minister of Health, H.E. Humaid Mohammad Al Qutami at the Dubai International Convention and Conference Center. I returned so excited by that trip that I had to write about it. Thus, you are being treated to my notes and observations of that trip!

Before I left for my trip, I remember a student asking me how on earth the Feng Shui of a place like Dubai could be evaluated. As most of you will know, Dubai is quite a desert-like place and is largely flat, with very little land contour. Typically for almost completely flat areas (and from the pictures here, you can see it is quite flat), we use a Classical Feng Shui landform assessment technique known as 'Flat Land Dragon," which I will explain below.

Now when in Dubai, one cannot NOT check out the most famous hotel in the world, the self-proclaimed 7-star Burj Al Arab or Tower of the Arabs Hotel, which has hosted celebrities such as golfer Tiger Woods, tennis players Andre Agassi and Roger Federer and a bevy of Hollywood celebrities the likes of Tom Cruise, Brad Pitt, Naomi Campbell and Angelina Jolie. Built on a man-made island, the Burj Al Arab is the tallest building in Dubai, and the tallest hotel in the world. It is an architectural icon and engineering wonder and is also one of the most luxurious hotels in the world with over 8,000 square metres of 22-carat gold-leaf!

And of course, the Burj has some truly fascinating Feng Shui features. So, I obviously cannot NOT share with you my observations on the external Feng Shui of the Burj Al Arab!

When in Flatland, a Protrusion is worth Ten Thousand in Gold

又再笑談風水

The first thing when it comes to looking at the Feng Shui of such a large structure is to consider the landform. Because this is a completely flat area, the Flat Land Dragon principle applies. According to classical Feng Shui principles, when the land is completely flat (Yang), then the tallest structure (mountain - Yin) that protrudes, attracts all the Qi of the area. At 1,053 feet, the Burj is without a doubt one of the tallest hotels in Dubai and so it is clearly drawing in and converging the Qi in the near vicinity.

At 1,053 feet, the Burj is without a doubt one of the tallest hotels in Dubai and so it is clearly drawing in and converging the Qi in the near vicinity.

Now, it is one thing to have the Qi pulled in, but it is equally important to lock in the Qi properly. For this, you need to have an embrace. Check out the Google aerial image of the Burj and the photograph from the top observation deck of the Burj. There is a wavy structure on the left hand side of the Burj. This is the Jumeirah Palm Beach Resort, another very successful beach resort in Dubai. This structure acts as the left embrace or Green Dragon for the Burj, locking in the Qi from the left side.

Wild Wadi

Jumeirah Beach Hotel

Qi Mouth

A Google aerial image of the Burj. The Jumeirah Palm Beach Resort acts as the left embrace or Green Dragon for the Burj, locking in the Qi from the left side.

Next, we must look for an Ann Shan 案山 (Table Mountain) to help keep the Qi from escaping out through the front. In front of the Burj is the Wild Wadi Water Park. If you look at the picture taken from the front entrance of the Burj, you will notice there is a small hill (not the roller coaster). This acts as the regulating mountain for the Burj, to lock in the Qi that is being collected. This setup conforms to the Huge Door star shape. Those of you who have read up on these things will know that a Huge Door Star mountain is the star that governs prosperity.

Interestingly, right at the front of the Burj is a large fountain. This fountain not only serves to collect Qi at the front of the Main Door, but is also shaped like a Huge Door Mountain, mimicking the macro Feng Shui on a micro scale.

Intriguingly, the scenic bridge road that connects the Burj to the mainland has been constructed so that it is a gentle, meandering road (see Google aerial image) and also, it is not visible from the South-facing Main Door! And, it also comes into the building at the correct angle, which is *Sheng* Hexagram, thereby conforming to the Direct-Indirect Spirit principle in Feng Shui. This mirrors the macro Feng Shui, wherein there is a Qi mouth in the Southwest's *Kun* Da Gua Hexagram formed by the roads (see Google aerial map). It would seem the Burj's architects and designers avoided an important pitfall of having Sha Qi directed at the property, by making the road curved rather than straight and also, created a very nice Qi flow coming in at the correct Southwest direction.

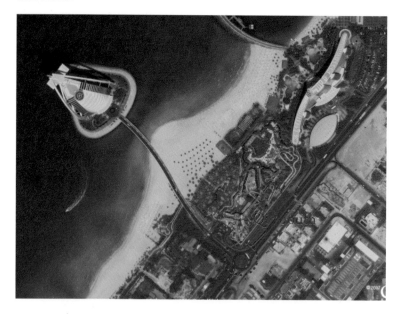

Now, a luxury hotel, and one that charges a minimum of USD 2,000 for a night's stay to boot, would definitely be an ambitious business venture to say the least. Well, guess what? The Burj is almost consistently fully occupied. But hey, with such optimised Feng Shui, it is hard to imagine the hotel doing anything but good business.

Did they, didn't they... Feng Shui It?

This is the 650 million dollar question indeed. Certainly, there is a tremendous amount of compliance with some of the key classical Feng Shui principles such as San Yuan's Da Ling Zheng and the landform principles. It is difficult to say if it was professionally done but that's not really the point. Whether it was accidental or deliberate, the fact of the matter is the Feng Shui at the Burj is pretty good!

However, the set-up is not perfect either, in my personal opinion. Improvements certainly could be made to improve the Burj's Feng Shui further, in particular, with regard to the problem of the lack of support at the rear of the structure, which exposes it to the Sha Qi from the sea. Generally, we like to have the building protected from Qi on all fronts and it is particularly important to have a solid backing at the rear of any structure, as this is what ensures longevity of prosperity and long-term success, as well as return-on-investment.

The Burj brings forth an interesting point about the idea of man-made Feng Shui. Most of you will know that I have consistently indicated that classical Feng Shui calls for natural objects in the environment. You have to have the mountain and water in the right location. Usually you cannot "make" mountain and water.

There is a small exception to this rule. Or perhaps I should say large exception.

And that exception is when you have the means and capability to control the structure of not just the building, but the land structure, a full one hundred percent. When you can build the structure from the ground up, including the land in which the building sits on (the Burj sits on a man-made island), and you control the surrounding areas around the structure (the Jumeirah Resort is owned by the same owner as the Burj) and money is no object, then, man-made Feng Shui is an option. But how many people have the money to buy enough sand and concrete to make a real mountain in their backyard or dig a river and attempt to control the elements through engineering feats? Very few indeed.

For most 'mere mortals,' man-made Feng Shui is not an option and simply not practical or feasible. So we have to rely on what nature has to offer, which can be a bit of a challenge, but not impossible.

又再笑談風水

A Room With a
Burj-Eye View

How does the internal layout of the
Burj Al Arab measure up on the Feng
Shui scale?

In a previous story, I talked about the
external Feng Shui of the Burj Al-Arab.
In this story, I'm going to take you inside
the hotel and show you how its internal
layout measures on the Feng Shui scale.

又再笑談風水

In Feng Shui, "inside" refers to the area immediately outside the main Door and inside the Main Door. So in the context of a hotel it would be the lobby; the area where the guests enter the hotel and the reception area where they perform their check-in.

It is important to understand that we only look at the inside after we've checked the outside. The external macro Feng Shui situation always ranks ahead of the internal or micro Feng Shui. You cannot make up for a poor external Feng Shui set-up, no matter how good the internal Feng Shui is and how much it complies with the principles of Feng Shui.

The external macro Feng Shui situation always ranks ahead
of the internal or micro Feng Shui.

Having a great Flying Star combination at the Main Door is nothing to be excited about if the Main Door itself is not receiving beneficial Qi because the area does not generate positive Qi, or Qi is obstructed from entry by negative forms, or if the property is simply in a direction that doesn't make Qi attraction and collection conducive, such as on a Death and Emptiness line.

The face that the hotel has the largest square footage of gold leaf, and contains items within the building made of gold, does not in any way affect the Feng Shui. It only adds to the opulence.

From the previous story, it's clear that the exterior macro Feng Shui of the Burj is pretty good. We now turn our attention to the Main Door, which is how the Qi enters the building.

Bright Hall No. 1: The Burj immediate reception area.

The Main Door: A Qi Mouth

Is there anything blocking the Qi from getting to the hotel via the Main Door? Or is there any negative formation affecting the quality of the Qi entering the property? There are no negative forms affecting the Main Door – the road that brings guests to the hotel is a curved bridge, not a straight T-junction or straight road that will bring gushing, aggressive Qi.

The fountain acts as a mini Table Mountain.

There is a small fountain in front of the Main Door that acts as a mini Table Mountain. It is shaped like a Huge Door Mountain (Ju Men 巨門). There are actually 81 types of Huge Door Mountains and this one, which resembles a volcano, is known as a Jade Pillow Huge Door Mountain or Yu Zhen Ju Men.

At first sight, it would appear as though the fountain is obstructing the Main Door. However, there is a spacious distance between the Main Door and the fountain (a necessity given that the guests are all being ferried to the hotel in stretch limos or Rolls Royces). And the little circle about it actually helps Qi to collect and circulate.

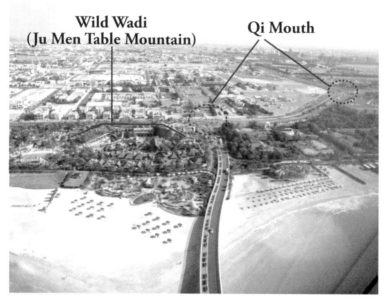

Positive curve: The road that brings guests to the hotel is a curved bridge, not a straight T-junction or straight road that will bring gushing, aggressive Qi.

The fountain is also an interesting feature because its position, by necessity, means the Qi is forced to enter the building through the Southeast and Southwest sectors, thereby conforming to the Indirect Spirit principle of San Yuan Feng Shui. This is also mimicked at the macro level, as there is a large intersection in the Southwest direction of the hotel. In Feng Shui, this is called the internal conforming to the external and is ideally what we would like to see in a large structure.

Bright Halls Aplenty

As you enter the hotel, it is clear that its layout conforms to the three internal Bright Halls requirement – according to the Feng Shui classic Ru Di Yan 入地眼 (*Entering Earth Eye Classic*), this is a Goldfish Ming Tang Formation or Goldfish Bright Hall Formation. This is simply poetic language and is meant to allude to the Qi flow being like the shape of a goldfish and to indicate that it slows in a meandering and sentimental way. It has nothing to do with the real fish itself.

The immediate reception area is Bright Hall number one. There are two large aquariums located at the Southeast and Southwest sections. Again, the Indirect Spirit formula is present on a micro scale.

Generally, a Feng Shui practitioner will not use Flying Stars Feng Shui for such a large structure. Flying Stars is actually inadequate as a system to handle such a large building. But, coincidentally, the positions of the two large aquariums are in the Facing Star #1 and Facing Star #8, so it is not too shabby.

If you saw images of the Burj on TV, you will probably have seen the atrium located above the lobby. This atrium is the tallest hotel atrium lobby in the world and is large enough to accommodate the 38-storey Dubai World Trade Centre building! So that's a pretty big Bright Hall, which is the second bright hall.

Style and Feng Shui subtlety

So where's the third Bright Hall? It's on each of the individual floors. Each floor has several suites on it and each of these floors features an individual check-in reception area. This is Bright Hall number three and it serves to collect the Qi on each floor. From the hospitality and Feng Shui aspects, this is a great set-up as it ensures that the guests feel relaxed.

My room at the Burj.

What about the rooms? Aside from the fact that they all boast of a fabulous view of Dubai, each spacious duplex-style suite opens to a small foyer (mini Bright Hall) and then to a very large, high-ceilinged living room. So the Qi flow from the check-in reception on each floor flows to the rooms unobstructed and then into the individual room's living room. Guests feel comfortable because the Qi is flowing freely from the entrance all the way into the rooms.

Of course, for a hotel the rooms are important but the administrative offices are the key to its ability to have and retain good, regular business. As a guest, that was not part of the hotel that I was shown, so I cannot speak for its business Feng Shui. I would say that an evident negative point is the main entrance to the hotel's spa on the 18th floor, which has less-than-ideal forms and is also located on a floor that doesn't quite correspond with Xuan Kong He Tu calculations.

I hope my two stories on the Burj Al Arab have in some ways helped to improve your understanding of Classical Feng Shui. So, if by any chance you are going to visit Dubai, be on the lookout for the subtle Feng Shui features that I've mentioned.

又再笑談風水

Have Luo Pan Will Travel

Often, I am approached by people at my seminars and talks who are very interested in Feng Shui, but are intimidated by the idea of lots of formulas and mugging information. Or they think it is a seriously complex field of study that is dry and extremely tedious. In fact, there's a lot of excitement and adventure in Feng Shui! Learning and researching Feng Shui is not about being trapped in a library full of dusty books or slogging away in a classroom. On the contrary, learning Feng Shui involves a lot of hands-on observation and yes, even adventure! That's why I encourage my students to Walk the Mountains and Chase the Dragons – to go out, look at the mountains and rivers, observe buildings and be curious about everything.

Up the mountain, down the river

Researching and studying Feng Shui is like being Indiana Jones - there are no rickety bridges to cross or gun-toting characters that cross our paths, but there's quite a bit of adventure, travel, and detective work involved. Finding and studying interesting Feng Shui formations have taken me to a lot of places that most people probably wouldn't go. Occasionally, it's quite exciting. Going to the rooftop of the world in Tibet in search of Heavenly Pool Water and breathing canned oxygen all the way just to get a glimpse of the unique High Level Dragons that are found in Tibet was definitely an adventure, not just for me, but also for my students who went there with me on that trip.

At the Lian Zhen Source Dragon Mountains in Tibet.

Sometimes however, quite a lot of detective work and legwork is needed to discover interesting Feng Shui spots and locations, especially those with historical significance. For example, searching for the Yin House locations of great leaders and historical figures in China takes a lot of effort. One time I took a group of my students to audit the Yin House Feng Shui of Chiang Kai Shek, the founder of Taiwan. In order to find Chiang's ancestral tombs (specifically that of his parents), I spent a lot of time tramping around the backwater and provincial areas of Zhejiang in China (braving the famous Chinese toilets!) and practicing my Mandarin by talking to the locals in order to ascertain the location of the ancestral tombs.

Researching Feng Shui also throws up a lot of red herrings, so one has to be not only a detective, but a combination historian-archaeologist as well, in order to piece together the information with the historical facts as well as with the snippets of information from the locals. Going to Chiang's ancestral home is often misleading if you're not familiar with the history of his family or don't pay attention to the little details. Many Feng Shui enthusiasts who visit the Chiang family home are usually not able to see why Chiang managed to rise up and become such a great leader. This is because while the Feng Shui of the Chiang ancestral home is reasonably good, with the forms showing a Literary Arts Star and a Tan Lang General Star at the Direct Spirit Location, it's not the sort of formation that can produce a powerful leader.

Assessing the tomb of Chiang Kai Shek's father.

又再笑談風水

The answer to the conundrum is rather simple. Chiang never made use of the Feng Shui in his ancestral home. He was not born in the family ancestral home (he was born in the family salt store), and while he inherited the ancestral home as the second son, he didn't live there. During his rise to power, Chiang lived in a different residence with his wife, Soong May Ling. Now, that home has a General Seat Star interlocking the Water Mouth, resulting in a Sleeping Bow Water (Mian Gong Shui 面弓水) Formation. The property is also flanked by Ju Men Mountains nearby, producing power, status and authority.

Chiang Kai Shek's birth place.

Looking without seeing

Let's say you're not into checking out Yin House Feng Shui and not into going around the countryside looking for the tombs of dead people. If you are into cosmopolitan cities perhaps, or you like shopping, you can also learn a little Feng Shui in your favourite locations. All you have to do is - look. Yes, just look!

Have you ever wondered what makes both the Oxford Street in England and the Champs D'Elysee in Paris highly sought out real-estate locations? Whenever I visit a new city on a research mission, I always make it a point to either take a helicopter ride or go up to a vantage point like a tower to have a look at the city and its central business districts or shopping areas. This gives me a vantage viewpoint of the macro landforms that are influencing the Qi of the area. After I've seen it from the top, then I walk around the area. I look to see the little hills in the distance, and undulating landscape of these areas and see if there's water coming in from the right direction. And the best part is: it never feels like work!

Why is the Champs D'Elysee in Paris a highly sought out real-estate location?

Even a visit to the mall can be an informative Feng Shui exercise. Ever wonder why a particular mall is perennially busy and others can barely get a decent crowd in on a weekend? Chances are it's not just the shops. It's the Feng Shui. Are there mountain and water forms in the vicinity? Or is it on a flat location? Does the mall appear dark and gloomy, even on a bright day and with plenty of windows to let in the sunlight?

又再笑談風水

In Feng Shui, it is important that buildings have natural light; otherwise, the building becomes very Yin. Now, logically speaking, having enough windows should enable the building to have natural light in abundance, correct? But if you visit certain malls or apartment buildings, it's still gloomy or very Yin despite having lots of windows. And it certainly doesn't put anyone in the mood for shopping.

Why does your favourite store seem to be floundering despite its great products or items? Take a look at the location. Is there a big lamp post at the entrance? Is it under the escalator? Is the entrance low, suppressing the door? The Main Door is an important aspect of the Feng Shui of any property because that is where the property receives its Qi. So we don't like any blockage at the Main Door.

Always pay attention to Main Doors of properties.

By observing and looking at the doors and main entrances, and looking at the roads and walkways, corridors and pathways, you can figure out how the Forms are affecting the Feng Shui of a property. And this is the same everywhere around the world – in Hong Kong, in Singapore, in Japan, in America, or in Europe. The forms always repeat themselves, whether deliberately or inadvertently. Even if you don't know how to fly the stars using Xuan Kong Feng Shui or if you aren't that good with memorizing formulas, just looking can be informative enough. Feng Shui doesn't have to be all serious and stuffy – it can be fun, and it can be an adventure too!

By observing and looking at the doors and main entrances, and looking at the roads and walkways, corridors and pathways, you can figure out how the Forms are affecting the Feng Shui of a property.

Playing Hide and Seek with the Dragon in India

As a Feng Shui consultant, most of the time I see clients and visit properties in full 'consultant regalia' – long-sleeved shirt, tie, leather shoes and sometimes a corporate jacket. Even when I'm visiting a construction site or a memorial park, I feel more comfortable in my normal consultant attire. But there comes a time (or a few times) in every Feng Shui consultant's life when roughing it out is required. And this was the case sometime back, when I was in India to follow up on a consultation engagement in a rural part of the country.

The location of the consultation was in the outskirts of Ranchi, which is about 4 hours by train from Calcutta. The actual site is a further 3 hours from Ranchi itself. Now, I am used to rural areas because I frequently have to visit such areas in China for research during my China Excursion trips with my students. But these rural areas in India are a lot more rural than rural China. We are talking about trekking country – we are talking about places where the roads are mud passages – we are talking about places where there isn't a village in sight for miles!

A Land Rover was provided for us to traverse the audit site, which covers 12,000 acres of virgin land. We were supplied a map, but as we soon discovered, the map was seriously outdated. Many of the cartographic markings were off, such as the location of the river. So, I was going to have to do this consultation much like the traditional Feng Shui masters of the ancient times. Except, thankfully, I wouldn't have to do it on horseback or on foot. A Rover and our driver, together with our client's representatives, would transport me and my assistants around.

Normally for such a large site, I request for expediency and speed, and ask that the client arranges for a helicopter sweep of the area as was the case during my last visit to a similar area on another consultation about one year ago. An aerial perspective usually makes things faster although the approach to sighting the Landforms is different and requires you to picture the Forms differently because you're viewing them from a higher perspective, as such. However, as it is the height of monsoon season now in India, a helicopter ride is not feasible (although for the 2 days I was surveying the site, it didn't rain a drop! I was thankful I selected a good date for this expedition).

Start at X

With 12,000 acres of land, we were to select a suitable location on which to build a power plant. To get an idea of how big this site is, the average American football NFL field is 1.322 acres. The site is big enough to house 9077 American football fields! It took us the better part of 4 days to survey the entire area. And then there is the question of how one actually begins to audit such a large plot of land. There was no "X marks the spot" on the map we were given.

The Snow Heart Classics 雪心賦 has a saying, "Look for the Water Mouth When Entering the Mountains, Seek the Bright Hall when you have reached the Meridian Spot," 入山尋水口，登山看明堂. So first, I would have to find the Water Mouth.

After hours of driving around, I noticed two distinct mountains that caught my attention. They looked like two lions looking at something in the distance. In the Classics, there is a line about a land formation called 'Great Beasts Facing the Meridian Spot'. Aha – we were finally onto something.

So off we went to look for what the mountain lions were looking at, which were two hills in the distance. I was sure we would find the Water Mouth there; even though there was nothing marked on the map to indicate the presence of water. Sure enough, as we reached the hills (after ploughing through some serious secondary jungle and very rough terrain), we found a stream. It was unmarked on the map as it was not a major river. The two Beasts were in fact the "Guardians of the Water Mouth" (Shui Koou Sha 水口砂) when viewed from the location of the stream.

Now, once we have found water, we have found the Qi mouth.

Now, once we have found water, we have found the Qi mouth. The Meridian Spot or Long Xue had to be not too far away. Immediately I looked around, again using the line of sight of the Water Mouth Guardians, and there it was, the Dragon Vein coming from a Rewards Star (Lu Chun 祿存) mountain that could only be perceived from the Water Mouth location. So off we went to the Vein to check out the quality of the vein and see if it was suitable for the client's needs. This required actual trekking through muddy ground.

At the vein, it was indeed a sight to behold. It is hard to imagine that deep in the rural heartland of India, one can see such incredible Feng Shui. The incoming Dragon Vein was at Geng Direction, with good penetration (Chuan Shan Long 穿山龍) into the land. It was supported by two Mountains – an Earth Door (Di Sha 地煞) and Heavenly Bright (Tian Gang 天罡) Mountains as the greater embrace.

The land itself is a Bowl Formation, which is a gently dipping area perfect for gathering Qi. There was a Huge Door Mountain (Ju Men Xing 巨門星) indicating good wealth prospects and excellent expansion and growth opportunities. On the opposite, there was a beautiful Ru Yi Table Mountain (Ru Yi An Shan 如意案山), which is also called the "Lying Down Wood Table Mountain." This serves to lock in the Qi and enable it to be tapped. Coupled with the Guardians in the distance to lock the Water Mouth, this site was looking really good.

The icing on the cake is that this site didn't just have good Feng Shui. The purpose of our expedition was to find a site suitable for building a power plant. This is a Fire element site. The Ru Yi is a Wood Element and the supporting rear mountain is an Earth element. Wood grows Fire, Fire produces Earth – this site could not be any more perfect for our client's needs. The natural formation must support the building and its function. This is the correct Feng Shui setup.

Ru Yi
Wood

Fire
Fire

Mountain
Earth

Of course, the project has a long way to go. As the client has control over every aspect of development on this land, including the location of the roads, entry points and building location, he will be able to plan the development to optimize the Feng Shui all the way. There will be date selections to be done for the ground breaking and also, the opening of the plant. It's a long way to go. But the toughest part, the most fun and challenging part - playing Hide and Seek with the Dragon - is done.

又再笑談風水

The Power
of a Good Date

In this article I give you a 'taster,' of sorts, of two pertinent issues related to Feng Shui: the power of picking a good date, and the BaZi analysis of a person who went out of control. Both stories highlight how 'hindsight is always 20/20,' meaning that everything seems clear when you look back on something and wonder, "Why didn't I see that coming?" Date Selection and BaZi are two effective tools to predict outcomes and give you an idea of what to expect before it comes, especially if used responsibly and in context. Here are just two examples why I say that.

It's all about a good date

While working on my book on Date Selection, I remembered my own experience starting off a venture on the wrong date (yes, believe it or not, we are so busy taking care of our clients' needs that we sometimes forget to select a good date for our own activities!). In hindsight, of course, it provides for a great example of how date selection matters and what a difference a good date can make.

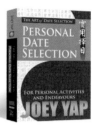

Some of the amazing sights in Tibet.

It was 2006 and I was preparing for my usual reconnaissance of the locations for my China Excursion course. This included going to Tibet, which I had planned to include in the 2007 Mastery Academy China Excursion. The trip, needless to say, was an absolute disaster. My team members all had serious altitude sickness of varying forms, and one team member got so sick that he had to be taken to a hospital for having water in the lungs, before being immediately flown out of Tibet to Chengdu. Naturally, the following year, as I took my students to Tibet for the annual Mastery Academy China Excursion, we took every precaution under the sun to make sure everything would be fine, including selecting a good date! Not only did no one get sick, but the entire group of students had a great time. So, why was one trip so disastrous and the other so smooth-sailing? It's all in the dates.

For my 2006 reconnaissance trip to Tibet, we departed on what is regarded in the 12 Day Officer System of Date Selection as a Balanced Day 平日. This is generally regarded as an acceptable date to commence long-distance travel. However, when the Dong Gong Method, another method of date selection, is considered, then the date that my team and I left for Tibet was actually a bad date because that was a day where a Fire Star was present and travels to the North would be affected by Black Sha Qi. Now, since we flew to Beijing and then onto Chengdu before heading to Lhasa, we were heading North the whole time. However, as I had gone from Hong Kong, I was somewhat less affected than my traveling companions who had traveled from KL. The exact date we landed in Tibet was a Stable Day (Ding Re 定日) according to the 12 Day Officer method but according to the Dong Gong Method, it was an inauspicious day, being afflicted by the Bing Fu illness star, which was exactly what happened!

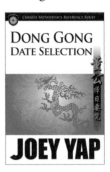

By contrast, the following trip, the Mastery Academy team and the students landed in China for the China Excursion on a Stable Day according to the 12 Day Officer System. Furthermore, based on the Dong Gong Method, this day had the Heaven and Monthly Virtue Noble Stars, the Yellow Spiral, Purple Sandalwood, Heavenly Emperor, Earthly Emperor and Golden Storage Stars. Not only was no one ill, but everyone had a good time and even the weather was fine.

In summary: that's the power of a good date!

China's great men and their tombs

During that trip, one of the sites I had selected for my students to audit in China was the tomb of Deng Xiao Peng's mother. Now you might be wondering - why aren't we looking at Deng's own tomb? Well, in Feng Shui, if we want to know why a particular person has achieved great things in their life, we don't look at their tomb - we look at the tomb of their ancestors. This is because Yin House Feng Shui affects descendants so if we want to know how someone is going to turn out, the answer is to check their parents' or grandparents' tomb.

And certainly, this explains the differing fortunes and destinies of two of China's greatest leaders: Mao Zedong and Deng Xiao Peng. Mao will always be immortalised in China as a great leader and first 'Modern Day Emperor,' while Deng, despite being one of the important leaders of the Communist Party of China, never held any official position as head of state.

Deng Xiao Peng's ancestral tomb.

This is because Yin House Feng Shui affects descendants so if we want to know how someone is going to turn out, the answer is to check their parents' or grandparents' tomb.

Mao's Yin House Feng Shui originates from his grandfather's tomb whilst Deng's is drawn from his mother's tomb. This is already a strong revealing indicator of the different paths the two men will take. In Feng Shui, it is said "Male is Yang, Female is Yin, Father is Bones, Mother is Flesh." Now, what does this mean?

"Mother is Flesh" refers to the use of Yin Qi, and talents and skills that are gained through experience, observation and through study. "Father is Bones" refers to what is already in you at the point of birth - latent talent or abilities and innate character. So Mao's leadership skills and charisma were in-born, whilst Deng had to learn the hard way how to rise to the top.

Between the two tombs, Mao's grandfather's tomb, atop a magnificent hill with a North Guardian (Bei Chen Xing 北辰星) locking in the Water Mouth of the area, is definitely superior to Deng's mother's tomb, which is a good but basic Five Petal Lotus Formation. Mao's grandfather's tomb has some of typical features of Emperor-creating formations, while Deng's mother's tomb derives its Qi from the Five Petal Lotus Formation itself. Deng's power is not just true power, but takes a long time to secure, just like the lotus takes a long time to emerge from the muddy waters. The bloom of the lotus also does not last, just as Deng's power did not hold sway for long.

Mao Ze Dong's ancestral tomb.

Both Deng and Mao's children did not succeed them to positions of great power and influence. This is because both the burial sites do not have multiple layers of incoming Dragons but a single meridian spot. This indicates power for only the immediate descendant, but not lasting power that carries through the generations and creates a dynasty. This is in contrast to the tombs belonging to the ancestors of the founders of the Ming and Qing dynasties, where there are extensive incoming Dragons and supporting mountains behind the main spot, indicating lasting power -12 generations down, to be exact.

Inter Locking Qi mouth at Mao's ancestral tomb.

What makes a person go berserk?

I received a flurry of text messages from my students when I was away in China, asking me about the BaZi of the young man who went on a rampage in Virginia Tech University in the US. Based on public domain information, I got his birth date and plotted the BaZi chart of Cho Seung Hui, the Korean gunman (time of birth not known):

Xin Metal born in Ox 丑 and Ox is part of the season of Winter. In BaZi, we have a phrase "water and metal too much emotion," and this chart epitomizes that. This young man was emotionally unstable. As he was born in Korea and migrated to the US, this move further affects his chart negatively since the direction of West is associated with the element of Metal. It would definitely have been better for his mental state to remain in Korea, in the East, which is Wood.

Based on the calculation of his luck pillar, he would still be in the Gui Hai luck pillar. This means that his Year Pillar is in a fu yin formation with his luck pillar. A fu yin refers to a sad crying event. His year pillar is not only in a fu yin formation, but there is also a self-punishment between his year pillar, his luck pillar and the annual pillar of 2007. Hence, this person was deeply emotionally affected and unstable in that year.

The fu yin also explains his suicide - it is often explained in ancient BaZi literature like the San Ming Tung Hui that a fu yin can bring about sad, self-destructive issues or even death. The Year pillar represents a person's external outlook and also, the feeling of gratitude. When this is affected, the person feels suppressed and disturbed. As the star affected is the Hurting Officer 傷官 Star, the person becomes rebellious, angry and desiring to prove the people around him wrong about their perceptions of him.

Of course, there's more to this chart, but in keeping with the taster theme, I'm going to keep it short and sweet. But this small glimpse conveys enough about the power of BaZi analysis in being able to predict outcomes of human behaviour.

Along with Date Selection, this is just two of the potent tools within the repertoire of Feng Shui and Chinese Metaphysics. I hope it's enough of a taste to enable you to want to savour more!

又再笑談風水

Ahoy Spidey, Dates Do Count!

Most people understand the importance of getting a good date to do certain activities like get married or hold an official opening. However, people often do not understand WHY having a good date is important. For most, getting a good date for an important activity is to fulfill some superstitious belief or to satisfy some cultural requirement (another box to be ticked off in the long list of wedding to-dos!).

又再笑談風水

I wrote this article sometime last year to show why a good date matters. And instead of picking an ordinary example like opening a simple business or getting married, I chose a very special industry, the movie business, to illustrate how a good date can make a difference. I selected this industry because I love movies, but more importantly, because there is no business like show business. In an industry where the cost of making a film seems to go only in one direction (upwards), the pressure for an expensive blockbuster film to open not just well but to sling home with a massive 'booty' within its opening 5 days is imperative. Losing money is not an option.

Also, Hollywood has always understood the power of a good date, although admittedly, not the kind found in the Tong Shu (Chinese Almanac). Traditionally, certain weekends are usually selected for the opening of the summer blockbusters such as July 4 or the US Memorial Day weekend. So this makes the comparison exercise with Chinese Date Selection methods a little more interesting!

The biggest two films that everyone was talking about last year were *Pirates of the Caribbean*: At World's End and *Spider-Man 3*. So for this Date Selection experiment, I used the *Spider Man* and Pirates trilogy. First, they both have common denominators – both the trilogies were made by only one director (so only one BaZi to reference) and secondly, all are 3-part films so it's possible to compare apples with apples. For the purposes of this article, I have used both the premiere date and the official opening date in the US (the date when screenings begin in theaters) to compare and contrast – the US date was chosen because the US market is arguably the most important market for the product. So, let's look at some of the basic details.

The Directors!

Spider-Man 1, 2 and *3* were directed by Sam Raimi. Raimi was born in the year of the Pig. His Day Master is Wu Earth. *Pirates 1, 2,* and *3* were directed by Gore Verbinski. Verbinski was born in the year of the Dragon. His Day Master is Jia Wood. (Birth data sourced from IMDB.com.)

The Dates

Let's look at the *Spider-Man* franchise first. *Spider-Man 1* opened on May 3, 2002 which is a Bing Zi Day. Using the 12 Day Officer Method (Jian Chu Shi Er Zhi Shen 建除十二值神), it is a Success Day. According to Grand Master Dong's System (Dong Gong Ze Re 董公擇日) of Date Selection, this is also a good day, with Yellow Embrace (Huang Sha 黃砂) and Sky Happiness (Tian Xi 天喜) stars present, along with the Heavenly and Monthly Virtue Stars. Spider-Man 2 opened on June 30, 2004, which is a Geng Chen Day. According to the 12 Day Officer Method, this is an Open Day. This date is also auspicious according to Grand Master Dong's System of Date Selection, with the Heavenly Success (Tian Cheng 天成), Yellow Spiral (Huang Luo 黃螺) and Purple Sandalwood (Zi Tan 紫檀) stars present. *Spider-Man 3* opened on a Full Day and an auspicious day according to Grand Master Dong's System. Interestingly, this date also contains Sam Raimi's personal Fame star and his personal Resource star, which might explain why despite less than great reviews, the film still made a killing on its first weekend!

All three of the *Spider-Man* films opened on what would be regarded as positive and favourable days for an official opening. Thus, the producers were rewarded with some nice box office gold!

Title	Opening Gross (US$)	Worldwide Gross (US$)
Spider Man 1	114 million	821 million
Spider Man 2	88 million	784 million
Spider Man 3	151 million	(n/a)

With *Pirates of the Caribbean*, all three of the films had a separate premiere date and an official opening date. With all three of the Pirates films, the film either had a good premiere date and average opening date, or an average premiere date and a good opening date.

For example, *Curse of the Black Pearl*, the first installment of the *Pirates* trilogy, had its premiere on a Gui Wei Day in 2003. The day is in a Fu Yin relationship with the year – not good. However, the film opened on a reasonably good day according to Grand Master Dong's System. June 28, 2003 was a Ren Shen Day and a day that contains the Heavenly Fortune and Sky Happiness Stars. It was not an exceptionally good day but it was not too bad.

This might explain why the film had a rather slow start with a poor opening weekend gross (a mere US$46 million) but went on to a pretty decent worldwide gross of US$655 million.

By contrast, *Dead Man's Chest* had its premiere on an exceptionally good day with the Heavenly Fortune and Sky Happiness Stars present. The film opened on July 7, 2006, which is Full Day according to the 12 Day Officer Method, although it is not a good day when Grand Master Dong's Method is considered as it contains the Nine Earth Ghost star. However, this film not only had a fantastic opening weekend, grossing US$100 million in 2 days, but also holds the record for the highest opening weekend gross (US$135 million) and a staggering US$1 billion worldwide gross!

Title	Opening Gross US$	Worldwide Gross US$
POTC: Curse of the Black Pearl	46 million	655 million
POTC: Dead Man's Chest	135 million	1 billion
POTC: At World's End	114 million	(n/a)

Source: www.the-numbers.com

How did *Pirates of the Caribbean 3: At World's End* fare against *Spider Man 3*? Pirates had its premiere on May 19, 2007, with official screenings beginning midnight May 24, 2007. The premiere date is still a usable date according to Grand Master Dong's System but the ancient text says: "*Even though this day has the Sky Happiness and Heavenly Success stars, there is also the Red Phoenix and Grappling Hook Stars. Using this day will attract legal problems and disputes. It will also attract petty people.*"

The film's official US opening was a Remove Day, but is had auspicious stars, like the Yellow Embrace. However, there was also a negative star, the Heaven and Earth Drilling Sha, which made it unsuitable for significant events, according to Grand Master Dong's System.

Interestingly, Disney, producer of the *Pirates* films, is engaged in a spat with Sony, producer of *Spider-Man*, over who's opening weekend numbers are better! Talk about petty people! And the film's opening weekend has not been as good as its second installment.

Of course, this is a very simple computation of the dates used, involving very basic methods like the 12 Day Officer and Grand Master Dong System. To really evaluate the superiority of the dates, the key cast members and the investors as well as the studio heads' personal BaZi must be considered, and even the time of the first screening should be taken into account.

A more sophisticated Date Selection system like the Heavenly Star (Qi Zheng Si Yu 七政四余) or Mystical Doors (Qi Men 奇門) system could be used to further refine the dates. A Date Selection Specialist would not just select the dates for the opening in the US but also in every country if possible, and at the same time ensure that both the opening screening AND the premiere are held on good dates! What IS interesting from this little experiment is that in the instance of all six movies, none opened on bad days such as Destruction or Close Days. All six films had good dates, some obviously better than others. Perhaps, Hollywood understands the power of a good date in more ways than one!

A more sophisticated Date Selection system like the Heavenly Star (Qi Zheng Si Yu) or Mystical Doors (Qi Men) system could be used to further refine the dates.

又再笑談風水

The Other Art of War

Most Asians are familiar with the name Sun Tzu and his famous treatise, *The Art of War*. Sun Tzu is now also a familiar name in the Western world, with *The Art of War* having gained great popularity amongst the corporate circles in the late 80s and early 90s. Many Western military academies also teach *The Art of War* as part of their syllabus. But very few people know about the 'other' Art of War that comes from Chinese Metaphysics. It is called Qi Men Dun Jia 奇門遁甲 or loosely translated as Mystical Doors Escaping Technique.

Qi Men Dun Jia (or Qi Men, the common abbreviated name used by students of Chinese Metaphysics) is a Chinese Metaphysical study that was largely utilised in ancient China for warfare. Many famous military strategists in Chinese history, like Zhuge Liang of the Three Kingdoms Era and Liu Bo Wen of the Ming Dynasty, used Qi Men in their quest to achieve military supremacy for their emperors. Qi Men Dun Jia is a technique for calculating time and space that has been around for the last 3,000 years. It is used to pinpoint the exact and precise moments in time during which to undertake a specific action, hence its popularity in military strategy and military campaigns in ancient China.

Qi Men Dun Jia is a technique for calculating time and space that has been around for the last 3,000 years.

Now, if you are a Feng Shui enthusiast, you may have heard of Qi Men. You may even have heard that it has certain 'occult' elements to it, or that it is so powerful that it can enable a person to escape fate and destiny. Some books and Chinese Metaphysics teachers go so far as to claim that Qi Men can change matters of life and death. Some people even say that Qi Men is not a 'legitimate' field of Chinese Metaphysics because it can be used for illegal acts such as killing someone and getting away with it.

In short, Qi Men has a lot of baggage, mystique and an almost magical aura about it. And that's always a little dangerous in my view because it's then easy for people to be taken in by false claims about what Qi Men can do or to be apprehensive about learning Qi Men (because of the baggage about so-called occultism or non-legitimacy). So I'm going to share with you some straight facts about Qi Men so that you can better understand what this 'Mystical Doors Escaping Technique' is all about. But first, some background story.

You say Oracle, I say Kray Computer

About 2,000 years ago, only shamans and oracles could forecast things like rain and snow and tsunami. Well today, we use computers to do that. Computer modelling, using collected data on weather conditions and preconditions, helps us engage in metrological forecasting to predict all kinds of movement on Earth. If you think about it, the computers and devices that measure waves, cloud movement, sonic activity and tectonic plate movements are essentially tracking energy patterns and movement. Even the outcome of human activity today is being modelled and computed to predict outcomes – financial markets use sophisticated mathematical models to project stock movements or determine market fluctuations.

又再笑談風水

In the old days in ancient China, Imperial Astrologers didn't have Kray Computers or an Imperial Tech Geek working for them to come up with computer formulas to predict outcomes. Probably they didn't need it since they had the three Oracle Methods: Tai Yi Shen Shu, Liu Ren Shen Ke and Qi Men Dun Jia, which were used to forecast or predict outcomes in relation to aspects of time and space.

Tai Yi was used to divine the big events that happen on a large-scale within countries, such as earthquakes, big hurricanes, massacres and natural disasters. With modern technology this method has obviously become less relevant. Liu Ren was mostly used to divine the outcomes of daily personal events – but due to the pace of life in the 21st century where people are often making decisions every ten seconds, Liu Ren's usage is mainly limited to important major decisions. Qi Men was generally used for military activities, and largely used to determine not just the right time to act (attack the enemy) but what to do (attack where) and when to undertake that action (when to attack). It remains highly relevant today and I'll explain to you how it's used in the modern context.

All three of these techniques are not that much different from all the computerized modelling that takes place today. It's just that what is computed is not seen as synonymous with those ancient techniques. Personally I think it's a case of "I say po-tay-to, you say po-tah-to." Techniques like Qi Men compute energy patterns and movements – in that respect, financial market modelling or metrological weather prediction is no different. It is about computing patterns and movements. While financial market models use numbers, Qi Men uses Metaphysical Energies.

What ties Qi Men to Chinese Metaphysics and makes it 'legitimate' is the same base it shares with all the other aspects of Chinese Metaphysics. Qi Men is also rooted in the Heavenly Stems and Earthly Branches – the 'Jia' in Qi Men Dun Jia is actually a reference to the first of the Heavenly Branches, Jia. The He Tu, Luo Shu, 9 Palaces, the 9 Stars, The Constellations, the 8 Directions, the principle of the 5 Elements, and of course, Yin and Yang also all form the basic principles of Qi Men. It is a slightly more expansive system because it actually combines both the energy computation that we associate with Feng Shui with the astronomical calculations associated with BaZi, or Zi Wei.

Chinese Cosmic Chess

The name 'Qi Men Dun Jia' can be deconstructed into the following:

'Qi' does not refer to the energy Qi but instead to the mysterious, the strange, and the unusual. It is similar to 'Xuan' in Xuan Kong. It is a reference to the universal rules of the cosmos.

'Men' in direct translation refers to 'door' or 'gate.' Its actual meaning relates to a location or a direction. The core of Qi Men Dun Jia is about finding the right location or direction in which to commence an action or begin to do something. 'Dun' means to hide or escape or to keep hidden. 'Jia' is a reference to the first of the ten Heavenly Stems. 'Jia' here is a coded reference to the leader or the General (if applied in the battlefield).

When put together, Qi Men Dun Jia in literal translation is 'Mysterious Doors Hiding the Jia.' It's a bit of a mouthful and rather complicated-sounding, which is why I prefer to call it Mysterious Doors Escaping Techniques.

又再笑談風水

In many respects, Qi Men is like chess. In chess, the goal is to always protect the King but also to advance it. Hence you have the Rook, the Bishop and the Queen, which are often used in combination to protect the King and also, to advance the pieces. In Qi Men, depending on what you want to achieve, you essentially either want to hide the Jia or find the Jia in the Qi Men chart.

Qi Men Dun Jia itself has four different schools. These are all simply different approaches to Qi Men, similar to San Yuan or San He in Feng Shui. Qin-Dun (Astrological Qi Men) focuses mainly on the cosmological aspect of Qi Men and mostly uses the Constellations and Astronomy. San Yuan Qi-Men (Three Cycle Qi Men) is the most commonly-taught form of Qi Men and is used in tandem with Feng Shui and Date Selection. Fa Qi Men is somewhat unconventional in its use and is mainly associated with Daoist spiritual masters. Finally there is Flying Palace Small Qi Men, or Fei Gong Xiao Qi Men, a modified stripped-down version of Qi Men that is popular in Taiwan.

Qi Men can be used to analyse and compute outcomes at many levels ranging from yearly forecasts to hour-based forecasts. Most Qi Men practitioners either will use what is known as the Leaning Palace Method or the Flying Palace Method to engage in analysis of the Qi Men chart. There are up to 1,080 Qi Men charts, all which can be used to compute outcomes and pinpoint moments in time for specific actions and activities with a specific outcome.

又再笑談風水

Door to a magic kingdom?

In this piece I want to share with you a little about how Qi Men Dun Jia 奇門 遁甲 is deployed in modern times and how it is used by some of today's Feng Shui consultants.

Qi Men is essentially a system that breaks down the essence of time. The Qi Men system computes the energy present in the environment during each year, month, day and hour and represents it in the form of a Qi Men chart, which comprises 10 Heavenly Stems, 9 Stars Doors and 8 Doors. The goal is to pinpoint not just the timeliest moment in time in which to

又再笑談風水

undertake an action, but also to undertake that action from the correct location and direction to produce a specific outcome. It is this emphasis on location and direction that gives Qi Men its association and connection to Feng Shui.

Knowing when to do something, and which direction to approach the action and selecting the appropriate action based on outcome, is the epitome of 'doing the right thing at the right time'. Those of you who have read my book *The Art of Date Selection* will appreciate that 'doing the right thing at the right time' is very much the basis of Date Selection. The Chinese of course, must always go one step further – with Qi Men it's not just 'do the right thing at the right time', but 'do the right thing at the right time, that produces the right outcome'! This is why one of Qi Men Dun Jia's primary uses in modern Feng Shui consulting practice is for Time Selection.

do the right thing at the right time, that produces the right outcome

The Golden Moment

What is Time Selection and how is it different from Date Selection? Time Selection essentially refers to finding the right point in time to undertake an activity or endeavour. Now, conventional Date Selection methods which use the Dong Gong and 12 Day Officer systems incorporate Time Selection as well. But conventional Date Selection only involves the hour, once the date is verified as auspicious and favourable for that activity.

Pure Time Selection, for which Qi Men Dun Jia is used, ignores the date. Qi Men's techniques enable us to find a real 'golden moment' – an hour in a day combined with a specific direction and a specific action that can successfully be undertaken irrespective of whether or not it is a good day, and based on conventional Date Selection methods. In short, it could be the worst day of the year, but with Qi Men, it is possible to pinpoint one specific hour, and one specific direction, that will enable a particular action to succeed.

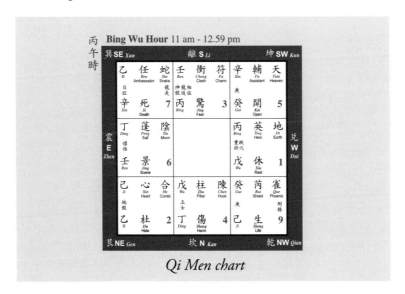

Qi Men chart

Time Selection in the modern context can be utilised for many activities. Relationship-related activities such as business meetings, negotiations or personal relationship matters such as a proposal are within the scope of Qi Men Dun Jia Time Selection. It is also used for wealth-related activities such as collecting debts or making payments for investment purposes or even something as straightforward as applying for a loan. Qi Men can also be applied to more conventional activities like sitting for an exam or submitting a thesis, or for career-related activities like applying for a promotion or raise, seeking a job or succeeding in an interview. Given its war strategy origins, it is also very useful for those in the political arena, wherein timing one's actions is essential.

In some of the instances above, the Qi Men Dun Jia practitioner will first plot the Qi Men charts for the relevant hours in the day. So, for example, a person wants to attend a job interview to be held in the afternoon. The Qi Men practitioner will then plot all the Qi Men charts for the afternoon. The person will then be told what time they must depart for the interview, and preferably in which direction they should approach the building.

Qi Men Dun Jia is generally considered a specialized field in Chinese Metaphysics and understandably, not many Feng Shui practitioners include Qi Men in their repertoire of skills. For the modern day Feng Shui Consultants who are trained in Qi Men, they usually use it as a supplementary technique to Feng Shui, as for example in Date Selection where the Qi Men technique can be used to help clients refine the selection of a suitable date in which to move into a property, or to commence renovations.

Changing the course of history?

In Hong Kong and Taiwan, many books on Qi Men Dun Jia are focused on the use of Qi Men for less than kosher activities like committing bank robberies or evading escape or criminal activity. People tend to forget that these books are usually written 'after the fact' and unfortunately, it tends to contribute to the belief that Qi Men is an 'occult' or deviationist technique and school. Such is the scary reputation of Qi Men that some Masters have conveniently used this as a "justification" for not teaching Qi Men to their students!

The secretive and mysterious nature of Qi Men is more likely due to the effectiveness of Qi Men, rather than its ability to be used for less-than-legitimate activities. Since it was such a handy and useful technique, the ancient Imperial families naturally wanted to keep it to themselves. Outsiders assumed that this was because it was deviationist (rather than just too good a secret to share), and that's how Qi Men got its deviationist tag.

Theoretically, Qi Men can be used to change the course of history. I want to emphasise the word 'theoretically.' Yes, a person pursued by a mob of 10,000 people screaming for his blood, could probably try to use the Escape Door (one of the 8 Mystical Doors) of the hour. But, when you're running for your life, who has time to plot a Qi Men chart (and it does take a good 15 minutes!) and then run in the right direction? You're just too busy running!

This is just like how, theoretically, Qi Men can be used to help you find a parking lot in an over-crowded mall. By the time you've plotted the chart for the hour and figured out where to drive, you probably would have found a parking lot! So the idea of Qi Men for use in deviationist activities is sound in theory, but honestly, not possible to undertake in reality.

Qi Men and Feng Shui: The Difference?

There is a great deal of overlap between Qi Men and Feng Shui when we look at the purpose of these fields. Both are focused on the use of time and space to help a person achieve their goals. Both Qi Men and Feng Shui focus on direction and location, and have predictive aspects that enable users to ascertain the outcome of specific actions. The difference is very much in the quality of the outcome (Qi Men is more specific) and also, the time needed to produce the outcome.

One advantage Qi Men has is that it generally produces quicker results – it can be almost immediate at times, depending on the circumstances. Feng Shui usually requires a few weeks or a few months before a positive or desired outcome can be seen.

However, because it was developed for battle-field situations where the facts and circumstances are constantly changing, Qi Men is less suited for achieving stable and continuous results. Stable and continuous results are what we usually prefer for business owners or home owners because typically they are interested in long-term results. It's also a little bit impractical to tell clients to keep changing the door that they use or the time they have to leave their house to go to work every morning!

Qi Men is suited to situations where movement is involved such as travel or a specific personal action. It is not restricted by physical environmental considerations, unlike some Feng Shui charts. Qi Men is not dependent on external Landforms. But if the activity or endeavour doesn't really involve that much movement or travel, or is a long-term effort, then Qi Men is probably not the best technique to deploy.

Feng Shui requires a tie in with the residents based on their Gua or their BaZi. In this respect, some set-ups may only favour one or two members of a family or individuals in a company. Qi Men is less dependent on Gua or BaZi and can be used to find a suitable time and direction for every member of the family or every key man in an organization to undertake a specific task.

While it's good to appreciate differences between Feng Shui and Qi Men, it's important to recognise that these differences don't denote superiority or inferiority. It simply indicates to us that in some specific circumstances, Qi Men is the better method, and in other circumstances, classical Feng Shui techniques may better serve the client's needs.

又再笑談風水

The San Yuan System of Feng Shui

There are two schools or 'pai' of Feng Shui, San He and San Yuan. These two schools are, if you like, the Oxford and Cambridge (or Yale and Harvard) of Feng Shui. They constitute two different approaches to Feng Shui. All systems and methods of Feng Shui can be classified under either one of these two schools.

又再笑談風水

Here, I'm going to delve a little more into the San Yuan system. At the beginner level, most people would have come into some contact with San Yuan Feng Shui - this is because popular systems like Flying Stars Feng Shui (Fei Xing 飛星), Eight Mansions (Ba Zhai 八宅) and Xuan Kong Da Gua are subsystems of San Yuan Feng Shui. San Yuan is more focused on deriving a Qi map of the property being evaluated through calculation, with forms being secondary. By contrast, San He is much more focused on formations, with Qi calculations being used to support the landforms.

Three Cycles 三元

Let's explore some of the basics of San Yuan because there's often a lot of confusion about San Yuan's basic concepts, in particular, the concept of San Yuan itself, which means 'Three Cycles' in Chinese. The phrase 'San Yuan' is popular in many Chinese writings, as well as being a common term in various aspects of life, philosophy and history.

For example, in the days of the Imperial Court, San Yuan referred to the three Imperial positions: Zhuang Yuan(狀元), Bang Yan (榜眼) and Tan Hua (探花). In Taoist philosophy, San Yuan refers to Heaven, Earth and Water. For students of metaphysics, the three divisions of time itself – the 180 years sequence into the upper, middle and lower cycles and 60 Jia Zi – is known as San Yuan. In the study of classical Feng Shui, the cosmic trinity of Heaven, Earth and Man is also known as San Yuan. Hmm… so then what does San Yuan mean?

Those of you who have dipped into the Chinese readings on this subject may have heard the argument by certain Feng Shui writers that San Yuan refers to Time, Yin and Yang, and Location. This is a common mistake that many people, including professionals, make about San Yuan. Why?

Because ALL systems of classical Feng Shui are grounded in the basic concepts of Time, Yin and Yang, and Location. San He also considers the aspects of time (by virtue of the 28 Asterism, Sun Position and other planetary positions), while Yin and Yang are reflected in the principles of Mountain and Water. Finally, San He is definitely focused on Location as far as location of the Meridian Spot (Long Xue 龍穴) is concerned. So how can San Yuan alone refer specifically and only to Time, Yin and Yang, and Location?

In fact, the answer is quite simple. The basis for San Yuan Feng Shui is the concept of cycles. Cycles, or Yuan, permeate in all aspects of the application of San Yuan Feng Shui. For example, the Parent and Sons Hexagram Formation is known as the San Yuan Xuan Kong Hexagrams, in which the 64 Hexagrams are categorised into Heaven, Earth and Man groups. Each Yuan, or cycle in this case, takes on 8 sub-directions; 4 of which are Yang Guas and 4 of which are Yin Guas, thus yielding 64 Hexagrams.

Another example of cycles in San Yuan is how San Yuan perceives time. Time is analysed in cycles of 20 years. There are 9 Periods of 20 years, which make up 180 years; hence every 20 years we have a capital change in the Qi that influences the world. The 9 periods are further subdivided into 3 levels: upper, middle and lower cycles. The entire cycle of time in San Yuan Feng Shui spans 180 years.

The basis for San Yuan Feng Shui is the concept of cycles.

San Yuan Who's Who

One of the challenges when it comes to San Yuan Feng Shui is the issue of the classics. Historically, San Yuan is quite a 'young' school of Feng Shui although this, it could be argued, is due to the fact that the fascination and fixation with 'schools of Feng Shui' or 'pai' is a relatively modern development in the world of Feng Shui. In particular, it has become more prominent since Hong Kong masters made the move to start teaching Feng Shui to the public, rather than strictly adhering to the master-disciple system.

Those of you who have dipped into classical reading will be aware of the claim that Huang Shi Gong's *Green Satchel Classics* (*Qing Nang Jing* 青囊經), along with Grand Master Yang Yun Song's *Heavenly Jade Classics* (*Tian Yu Jing* 天玉經) and *Green Satchel Commentaries* (*Qing Nang Ao Yu* 青囊奧語) are the founding classics of San Yuan, containing all the key theories of San Yuan. However, Grand Master Yang himself never actually classified his work as being part of the San Yuan School. It was only the later masters who classified the *Green Satchel Classics* as being a part of the San Yuan School.

Probably the classical Master who can be said to have 'founded' or given prominence to San Yuan as a school of Feng Shui was Master Jiang Da Hong, a Feng Shui master of the late Ming, early Qing Dynasty era. Master Jiang popularized Xuan Kong Feng Shui and he also wrote a commentary text, *Di Li Bian Zheng* 地理辨正 that is now regarded as a key text by most San Yuan Feng Shui Masters.

又再笑談風水

Di Li Bian Zheng is not to be confused with another book, *Di Li He Bi* 地理合壁, which is a sort of collection of academic theses and commentaries written by various Feng Shui masters from the Ming and Qing Dynasties, focusing mainly on the Flying Stars system.

People often confuse the two books or assume that *Di Li He Bi* was written by Grand Master Yang Yun Song. It was not. Master Jiang Da Hong's text remains the definitive San Yuan text that is a 'must read' for all those seeking an appreciation of San Yuan.

Why am I harping on about the classics and who started the school or 'pai'? It is important to understand who the 'founding fathers' of a school or 'pai' are because sometimes, it is the foundation for a practitioner's or master's claim of lineage. Hence, when it comes to San Yuan, any practitioner who claims to come from a long lineage of San Yuan masters is probably exaggerating the claim a little since San Yuan's lineage itself is quite short, beginning at best, in the late Ming era.

The Hallmarks of San Yuan

The calculation of Qi with reference to time is the main focus of San Yuan Feng Shui. The changes and influence of time and its impact are tracked to determine how the Qi has changed during the course of the period. Formulas, derived from the mathematical model of the Ba Gua, He Tu, Lo Shu and 8 Trigrams, co-referenced against the North Dipper 9 Stars, is the foundation for San Yuan Feng Shui.

The calculation of Qi with reference to time is the main focus of San Yuan Feng Shui.

While San He has a greater emphasis on the external forms, San Yuan has a more balanced approach to internal and external Feng Shui. San Yuan also considers time as a more important factor when compared to San He's approach. San Yuan also places a great deal of emphasis on the 64 Hexagrams in its application. Amongst the more popular San Yuan techniques include Xuan Kong, Eight Mansions and Dragon-Gate Eight Formations. These are full-fledged systems in their own right, but are seen as being 'allied' with San Yuan.

The popularity of San Yuan can be said to be due to the popularity of Flying Star Feng Shui and Eight Mansions, both of which are systems allied with San Yuan and are relatively easy for beginners to learn. San Yuan is also preferred these days because it is a more dynamic form of Feng Shui and suits the demands of modern society, which is all about quick-quick-quick results. Which system is better? Both have their strengths and it depends a lot on what your goal is. San Yuan is technically better for quick, short-term outcomes while San He is better for long-term set-ups (like say, if you are building a castle or planning an empire!).

I'd like to end this by suggesting that in today's modern world, a good Feng Shui practitioner is one who is neither dogmatic about practice (in other words, knows BOTH San He and San Yuan just as well) and understands that at the end of the day, the systems don't really contradict each other at an advanced level. It is not a case of which is better or more popular than the other, but rather, which system better suits the needs of the client and the demands of the property at that specific point in time.

San Yuan is also preferred these days because it is a more dynamic form of Feng Shui and suits the demands of modern society, which is all about quick-quick-quick results.

The School of Forms

Most of you have probably heard (by now!) that there are two schools of Feng Shui. The concept of 'school' is used as an English interpretation of the Chinese word 'pai 派'. In Feng Shui, like in many Chinese arts (such as Qi Gong or Kung Fu) there are 'pai' or groupings. These groupings are usually based upon a certain method, technique or approach to a field. When Bruce Lee developed his own form of Kung Fu, known as Jeet Kune Do, he was essentially establishing his own 'pai' or group. In that sense, the word 'school' in the context of 'school of thought' does to a degree capture the concept of 'pai.'

One incorrect and highly misleading interpretation of the two schools of Feng Shui is that they comprise the 'Compass School' and the 'Forms School.' In fact, all methods and techniques of Feng Shui use Forms and a Compass or Luo Pan. A more appropriate and correct division of the two schools of thought in Feng Shui is that Feng Shui methods and techniques fall into either a Forms School (Xing Shi Pai 形勢派) or a Qi School (Li Qi Pai 理氣派). There are two famous 'schools' that advocate Xing Shi and Li Qi, and these are the San He 三合 (Three Harmony) and San Yuan 三元 (Three Cycles). Most major Feng Shui systems, methods and techniques will fall under either one of these schools.

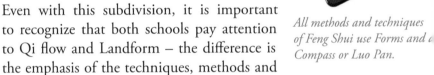

Even with this subdivision, it is important to recognize that both schools pay attention to Qi flow and Landform – the difference is the emphasis of the techniques, methods and

All methods and techniques of Feng Shui use Forms and a Compass or Luo Pan.

formulas. Generally, San He favours landform assessment over Qi assessment, whilst San Yuan favours Qi calculation over landform assessment.

I'm going to delve in depth into the San He School – the aim here is to provide you with a clearer understanding of what this particular school of Feng Shui is all about. Thus, when you engage a Feng Shui practitioner, you will be able to appreciate the methods he is using, gain a basic understanding of why certain changes or suggestions are made, and appreciate what the Practitioner is trying to achieve. I am also going to talk about some of the common fallacies and misinterpretations of San He principles so that those of you who are interested in Feng Shui and who read up on it on your own can separate the false theories or incorrect interpretations from the real explanations.

A San He Luo Pan (compass)

Now you might be wondering – do I need to know what technique my Feng Shui practitioner is using? After all, most people don't know anything about plumbing when they hire a plumber. Well, you may not need to know the subject to the level of depth of a practitioner but by understanding the methods and techniques you will be in a position to understand why certain changes are requested. In my own practice, I find that when clients appreciate why they are being asked to do something, compliance is usually easier to achieve. Also, it makes it easier for members of the public to distinguish between New Age practitioners and Classical Feng Shui practitioners.

Methodology and Approach in San He Feng Shui

San He is one of the oldest Feng Shui systems in practice. Famous advocates and masters of this system include Great Grandmaster Yang Yun Song (Tang Dynasty) 楊筠松祖師, Zeng Wen Shan 曾文辿, Jing Dao He Shang 靜道和尚 and Lai Bu Yi 賴布衣. The foremost texts for San He practitioners, written by Grand Master Yang, are the *Han Long Jing* 撼龍經 and *Yi Long Jing* 疑龍經. However, there are also some other important texts on San He that form the core readings required for any San He mastery, including *Yu Sui Zhen Jing (Jade Essence Classics) Ru Di Yan* 入地眼 *(Entering Earth Eye)* and *Xue Xin Fu* 雪心賦 *(Snow Heart Classics).*

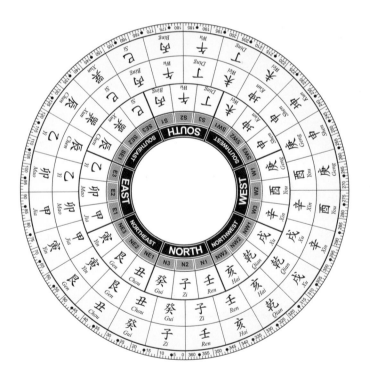

The 24 Mountain Ring of the San He Luo Pan.

San He methods focus on five factors – Long 龍 (Mountains), Sha 砂 (mountain embrace), Xue 穴 (Meridian Spot), Shui 水 (water) and Facing (Xiang 向). San He focuses largely on techniques of analyzing external Feng Shui. The methods are largely focused on appreciating and understanding how landforms generate and concentrate Qi, identifying the Meridian spot (Long Xue 龍穴) through evaluating the land contours and ascertaining where the Qi has concentrated by inspecting the formations in the land. San He, in that sense, is focused on observation of the land first, before moving onto the calculations of Qi for the interior of the property.

San He focuses largely on techniques of analyzing external Feng Shui.

Another distinctive principle of San He is the concept of Three Harmony. What is Three Harmony? It involves applying the Earthly Branches Three Harmony (which talks about the Mountain ranges in the vicinity) in tandem with the Water Formula Three Harmony that includes the 12 Growth Phases (Chang Sheng Jue 長生訣) and the systematic alignment between environment, house, and man.

Some typical methods for analysis and application used by San He Masters includes Ba Sha Huang Quan 八煞黃泉 - 8 Killings Yellow Spring, Piercing Mountain 72 Dragons, Earth Penetrating 60 Dragons, 120 Gold Divisions, 12 Growth Water, Assistant Star Water and Land Embrace methods (Bu Sha Fa 佈砂法).

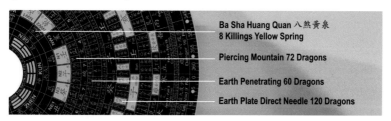

Ba Sha Huang Quan 八煞黃泉
8 Killings Yellow Spring

Piercing Mountain 72 Dragons

Earth Penetrating 60 Dragons

Earth Plate Direct Needle 120 Dragons

What system is my Feng Shui master using?

Okay, so you are aware of the theory now but how do you know what method your Feng Shui practitioner is employing? Well obviously one way of finding out would be to ask him, but you can also tell by observing what he does during the audit.

A San He practitioner usually will focus on the external environment primarily, so if your practitioner studies the mountains in the vicinity of your property, the waterways in the area, and uses a San He Luo Pan, chances are that he is using San He as his pet system. Of course, the San He practitioner will not ignore the interior of the house or internal Feng Shui, but his foremost focus will be the environment.

His goal will be to determine how to best orientate the property to suit the surrounding Mountain and Water formations and to try and match the location of the Water and Mountains in the area to San He formulas. Do not be alarmed or think you are being conned if he doesn't recommend Water Formulas to you because remember, all these formulas require natural water formations to conform to the formula and if you don't have a natural formation that you are able to use, the practitioner will not tell you to force the situation by digging a canal or putting a drain around your house. Instead, a good practitioner will strive to work with what is already in the environment.

又再笑談風水

The Right Way to Handle Sha Qi

When I first began writing for publications, one of my earliest articles was on the topic of how people are easily frightened by Sha Qi, to the extent that everything sharp and pointy becomes a Feng Shui bogeyman. While identifying Sha Qi in an area is important, you can't really expect to live in a civilised place without some kind of pointy or sharp object somewhere in the vicinity of your property. So it is all a matter of knowing what you are looking at, and being able to make a judgment call on the Sha Qi in question. For this purpose, I want to revisit the topic of Sha Qi to emphasize some of the finer points – before you decide to get too afraid!

Consider Distance

Busy roads can be considered Sha Qi, especially if they cut in front of the house, or the property is located on the 'blade' of the road; meaning that the curve of the road points at the property rather than embraces it. However, there's no need to panic if such a road is located far away from your

Roads that pose a potential Sha Qi problem

property. If you have a road with busy, fast-moving traffic two metres away from your house, or if the road curves into your house right at the front gate, then you may have a problem. But if this road is a distance away and only visible if you really look for it, then you don't really have a serious Sha Qi problem. Immediacy is what concerns us when it comes to Sha Qi.

Take a look at these pictures. These roads are quite close to the property that I audited some time ago. But these roads do not create a Sha Qi problem for two reasons: firstly, they are quite far and also more importantly, they are not actually visible from the property. Hence, the property is not affected by these negative features because they are too far away to be of significance.

Roads that do not pose a problem

Does the Qi really Sha?

Sometimes, you can have a tall or menacing feature in the vicinity, like a water tower. Now, most people will think: "Aha, Sha Qi!" And then they will think that they must avoid buying a house near this feature or where the feature is visible. A tall, high, pointy structure can be Sha Qi but in some instances, it can also be a positive form. For example, this Water Tower here, rather than emitting Sha Qi, actually functions as a Regulating

This Water Tower acting as a Regulating Mountain

Mountain (Shui Kou Sha 水口砂) which guards and locks the water mouth and prevents Qi from escaping.

Sha Qi don't always go on pointy and sharp alone. Otherwise, we'd all have to stop using pens, avoid eating with chopsticks and hide our fingers in mittens. An object that emits Sha Qi is usually one that not only has sharp and pointy features but also looks menacing. Now, if you look at an electrical pylon, and compare it to the water tower, I'm sure you can see what I mean about 'looking menacing.'

Not everything pointy and sharp emits Sha Qi.

What's the Sha Qi pointing at?

Once, at the entrance to the property I audited, I saw this:

Sharp edge→

Descending Water

Now, you might be wondering: "Is it the staircase that is bad? Or the sharp corner?" Those of you who voted for the sharp corner, you are right. That's where the Sha Qi problem is. The staircase is not Sha Qi but is in fact a formation known as Cascading Water (Jin Tian Shui 進田水), and is a positive form. The sharp corner is a problem that warrants attention because it points at the Main Door of the house. As a rule, if you are looking at Sha Qi that affects a particular sector of the house, versus Sha Qi that affects the Main Door, the Sha Qi problem at the Main Door is a bigger headache and warrants more attention. This is because if Qi is obstructed or negatively affected at the Main Door, then it doesn't matter how good (or bad) the rest of the house might be - the house is already starting out on a negative equity position from the Feng Shui point-of-view. Of course, when the negative star like the #5 Yellow flies in a particular year, this might pose a problem.

What happens if there is Sha Qi but it doesn't affect the Main Door? If you are a little more knowledgeable about Feng Shui, you can check which sector is affected by the Sha Qi and then, by determining which Gua corresponds with that sector, find out if a family member will be affected. For example, let's say the sector Dui (West) is affected by the Sha Qi. Dui, amongst other things, represents the youngest daughter. So if your family has no girls and only boys, then the Sha Qi does not present a problem to your family members.

I hope the processes I have outlined here are able to give you some idea of how to find a good Feng Shui property, and that the pictures have been helpful in allowing you to visualise some of the key positive and negative Feng Shui features that can be found in an environment. I hope this helps those of you who have a keen interest in Feng Shui screen your own properties.

Of course, when you Feng Shui-It-Yourself, it may not be as good as a complete professional audit, where the consultant will also look at the direction of the Main Entrance (if it is a gated community or enclosed housing area), ensure conformity to Direct and Indirect Spirit principles in the macro and micro environment and personalise the Feng Shui to you and your family members. But remember, doing something is better than doing nothing.

If you can't afford a Feng Shui consultation, do what you can. You may not be able to find a superb property, but you can avoid an unfavourable location. Ultimately, Feng Shui is very simple - avoid the Sha Qi, find the Sheng Qi. If you can do the first one, you're already halfway there! If you can do both, then you're definitely already putting yourself in an advantaged position, Feng Shui-wise!

Ultimately, Feng Shui is very simple - avoid the Sha Qi, find the Sheng Qi.

Decoding the Destiny Chart

The Chinese have always had a fascination with the metaphysical subject of Destiny. It was this profound curiosity about man's path in life, the journey of a person, and 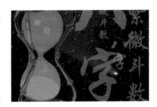 the question of who we are, why we are here, and what we are supposed to do during our brief time on this planet that led the Chinese to study and seek methods for analyzing a person's Destiny. These later evolved to become two systems of Chinese Astrology, BaZi 八字 (Eight Characters, also known as Four Pillars) and Zi Wei Dou Shu 紫微斗數 (Purple Star Astrology).

又再笑談風水

What fascinated the Chinese centuries ago remains one of the more enduring and continuing quests of mankind: to better understand ourselves, to better ourselves, and to appreciate what makes each unique and individual person tick. And, maybe, along the way, to figure out why is it that we've been put on this planet! Go to a bookstore and you will see a proliferation of books (and these days, tests), all attempting to explain to us, through scientific, psychological, biological, genetic or in some cases, just downright humorous ways, the question of WHO we are. And weighing down the shelves at another section called 'Self Help,' volumes and tomes attempting to tell people how to improve themselves beyond what and who they are.

The answers to these questions and many more, in fact, can be found through understanding a person's Destiny Code, or his BaZi.

So what is BaZi?

BaZi is a system of Destiny Analysis using a person's birth data, namely, his date and time of birth. The Eight Character BaZi chart is derived from the calculations of the elements prevailing at the time of a person's birth. This BaZi chart is a sort of Cosmic DNA, if you like. A BaZi chart is each and every person's individual and personal Destiny Code. Those Eight Characters contain a comprehensive, and arguably complete, collection of information about an individual and his life potential and capacity.

It may sound quite incredible but this is the genius of the Chinese Astrology system. A person's entire life - pitfalls, trials, tribulations, wealth, status, personality, characteristics, talents, abilities - are all encoded within these eight characters.

The BaZi consultant, who understands what the various codes mean within the BaZi chart, is then able to ascertain what kind of potential or capacity a person has in his or her life and also, is able to determine the person's luck cycle, which essentially indicates in which years he is likely to experience good luck, and in which years the luck is likely to be less than favourable. In short, by decoding a person's Destiny Code, a BaZi consultant is able to reveal what is in store for that person in their life, just as medical scientists can ascertain a person's eye and hair colour, and what types of medical illnesses they are likely to have, by analyzing their DNA.

BaZi and Feng Shui: Diagnosis and Prescription

At a professional practice level, BaZi and Feng Shui are essential complementary disciplines. Just like all doctors have to understand the biology of the body and the chemistry of drugs before prescribing treatment, all professional Classical Feng Shui consultants will have BaZi or Purple Star Astrology, another Destiny Analysis system, as a complementary or back-up skill to be used in tandem with Feng Shui. Some consultants will also use Face Reading or Mian Xiang as a third complementary discipline and back-up system.

Many people do not realise that it is extremely important that a person's BaZi is taken into consideration before his or her house or office is 'Feng Shui-ed.' Why is that? Well, before a doctor can write a prescription, he first needs to know what is wrong with the patient, right? Likewise, before a Feng Shui practitioner deploys his Feng Shui skills, he must first know and understand the problem he is trying to fix.

Some of you may have read or heard me say that Feng Shui is a goal-oriented science. The client, of course, must know what he wants to achieve with the use of Feng Shui. Sometimes, clients will tell me that they have a specific problem (for example, business relationships are problematic, or they find it tough making headway at work, or – the most common problem - not making enough money!). But most of the time, clients are

not certain as to what their problem is, or only have a vague idea of what the problem is. Hence, the Feng Shui consultant must check their Destiny Code before proceeding with the Feng Shui.

Money Money Money

Sometimes, the clients know what they want (like that Abba song, Money Money Money) but even in these instances, the Feng Shui consultant must still check the BaZi. Why? This is because Feng Shui is not some kind of cosmic steroid.

If you want to turn into Arnold Schwarzenegger overnight, steroids might help. But even then, you have to have the body and physical make-up that enables you to obtain those kinds of muscles. Similarly, if you want to turn into Warren Buffett overnight, Feng Shui can only help you if you have the Destiny to be a multi-billionaire in the first place. In other words, you must first have, before you can be!

In my Feng Shui classes, I always tell students: to perm hair, you must first have hair. This is in reference to the tapping of Qi in the environment. If in the first place the environment has no Qi, or no good Qi, you won't get superior results no matter how you try to tap into it or no matter what formulas you use. The 'to perm hair, first you must have hair' principle also applies to using Feng Shui to enhance Wealth or any other aspect of life. If you are not destined to be a multi-millionaire in your BaZi, or the potential for immense wealth is not there, then no amount of Feng Shui enhancement or super-powerful formula can make you one.

You must first have, before you can be.

What's the point in knowing if it's all bad news?

Some people are against the idea of knowing their destiny and take the view that life should be experienced as is. More often than not, people are against knowing their destiny because they believe that it will be self-fulfilling prophecy and limit them. I have also met people who take the view that they would simply rather not know anything about the future, because they are fearful of knowing what it holds.

It is not all bad news. In life, there is only one certainty, and that is death. In BaZi and Feng Shui, there is no such thing as 'totally bad' or 'totally good.' There is no end destination, there are only journeys. Some days the sea is calm, some days it is rough - so in knowing how the winds blow, you can steer your boat the right way.

Similarly, I disagree with the argument that BaZi creates self-fulfilling prophesies, limits people, or somehow encourages people to kill their dreams. In the old days, BaZi was used mainly to determine a person's fate. In other words, the focus was mainly on the hand you were dealt and simply knowing what kind of 'life' you would have. Of course, as a society we have come a long way from that mentality and present-day BaZi consultants approach this discipline in a very different way.

又再笑談風水

Today, BaZi is not only about knowing the hand that you are dealt, although that is part of the goal. It is about playing that hand as best as you can, to the best of your abilities. It is about understanding what you can and cannot do at certain points in time, and taking the right action to improve your life. It is about understanding yourself, and those around you, and then bettering your personal relationships, your opportunities, and your life.

BaZi tells you about your potential in life so that you can choose to do the right thing and avoid the disappointment that comes with wasting your time on an endeavour in which you'll have minimal success.

It tells you when disappointment strikes, when you should throw in the towel WISELY, and when you should continue to fight the good fight. It does not destroy a person's dreams; instead it points them in the direction of which dreams to chase because those are the ones that can become reality.

夢
DREAM

又再笑談風水

又再笑談風水

Breaking the Dan Brown Code

Dan Brown's *The Da Vinci Code* has
become a runaway literary bestseller since
the time it was published in 2003. Think
about it: how many people you know who
don't usually read bought a copy of the book
just because they had to know "what it was
about?" Regardless of whether the people you
know read the book and enjoyed it, the fact of
the matter is many others did – and it made
a huge success out of Dan Brown.

So without a doubt, I was curious enough to want to investigate his BaZi and decode his Destiny Code! So, first things first - Brown's chart looks like this:

Naturally, we are keen to understand the origins of his talent and you will find that his BaZi not only explains why such phenomenal and tremendous success has come to him in such a short time, but also why he has a keen interest in anagrams and codes and mysterious organisations like Opus Dei. It also tells us a little bit about why his previous attempts at songwriting and previous novels did not really go anywhere until *The Da Vinci Code.*

Before we proceed, a brief note for those readers who perhaps have little familiarity with BaZi, or do not know the terminology: Some of the terms are names that are directly translated from their Chinese names and so to the untrained ear will sound a little odd and perhaps create incorrect assumptions about what the term means, such as Seven Killings (sounds violent but take it with a bag of salt) and Eating God (no religious connotations or otherwise implied). If you are not familiar with BaZi, it is best to just assume these are special terms and to attach no impression or meaning to them. Of course, I will explain what the terms mean, so that you can appreciate how BaZi professionals decode a Destiny Code.

The Code of a Writer

In the study of BaZi, all charts have a structure. This is just like in Feng Shui, as a house's Qi map will also have a structure. Of course, there are common typical structures and there are unique structures. Brown's chart is a structure known as "Shi Shen Pei Yin Ge 食神配印格" or Output Matches Resource Structure.

In this chart, the Eating God star (represented by the Wood element) is extremely strong, having roots in the Chen 辰 (Dragon) and Yin 寅 (Tiger) branches of the BaZi. Jia Wood is also considered ideal for authors, especially when it is also the Eating God star. What is the Eating God star? At a superficial level of BaZi, Eating God represents amongst other things, a person's output or what they create. Individuals with Eating God also tend to be people who work unseen or are behind the scenes, such as an author.

Now, to be a successful author, you cannot just be able to write (otherwise, everyone out there who wrote would be a successful novelist). You have to have unique ideas, a special insight into the world, or great imagination and inspiration. In the study of BaZi, the Resource star relates to knowledge, inspiration,  and ideas while the star known as Indirect Resource 偏印 (Pian Yin) relates to unconventional ideas, unique perspectives and unorthodox thinking. Incidentally, these are just all the qualities needed for someone planning to write a novel full of codes, brain-cracking puzzles, and tricky anagrams involving the mystery of the century!

Imagination
Good ideas
Inspiration
Unique ideas

Now, in truly unique and special BaZi, the elements all work together and play off of each other. In Brown's Destiny Code, there is a perfect use of the Eating God star (represented by Jia or Yang Wood) because it is made useful by the Indirect Resource star (represented by Geng or Yang Metal). So, his writing is supported by good ideas. His Indirect Resource star in turn is of good quality because of the Ding Fire or Yin Fire found in the Horse 午 (Wu), located in the Month Branch of his BaZi. This Ding Fire or Yin Fire forges and makes useful the Geng or Yang Metal. Ding Fire or Yin Fire is the Direct Wealth star for Brown's chart. Direct Wealth, amongst other things, represents putting one's nose to the grindstone and working hard, and it also represents the Wife star for a man.

Of course, there are many authors out there - not all of them are worth an estimated 250 million. So does Brown's chart reveal his wealth potential? Yes. In the BaZi classic *Di Tian Sui* 滴天髓, a verse states: "How do you know if a person is rich, because he's born in the Door of Wealth." Brown's Wealth is represented by the element of Fire in his chart. The Month Branch of Brown's BaZi, the Wu 午 (Horse) is a strong Wealth star. Inside the Yin 寅 (Tiger) is also a Wealth star, an Indirect Wealth star, that is in Growth stage. Brown's Indirect Wealth star is Bing Fire or the fire of the sunlight, indicating that his Wealth potential from book royalties, like the fire of the sun, is infinite!

So, it can be said that in this BaZi, the individual has the potential and capacity to become a successful and wealthy author, and the Wife star is useful, helpful and of great significance.

Unlocking the Code

Brown met his wife in 1993, and they were married in 1997. In a newspaper article in The Observer, he is quoted as saying she is his 'inspiration.' She also has a big mention in his books and CDs (yes, before he wrote books, he wrote music, which is also an Eating God star activity). When he decided to become an author, his wife helped him get his first book deal, organized a book signing for his first book, did his PR, got him onto talk shows and helped him do a great deal of historical research for *The Da Vinci Code*. He has also stated in numerous interviews that his routine consists of getting up at 4 am to bang out the words in his loft. Talk about putting your nose to the grindstone!

His book is a bestseller although some reviewers complained about the awkward writing. A reviewer in The Guardian suggested that his writing made "a crisp packet read like a sonnet." Again the explanation is in the BaZi. Brown's Eating God star is represented by the element of Jia Wood. Jia Wood, in BaZi, is represented by tall trees. Trees grow only in one way and are straightforward and to the point. Hence, Brown's fuss-free, get-to-the point writing. It doesn't have to be beautiful to the ears, as long as you get the point!

> *But even within a favourable Luck Pillar,*
> *good luck does not come overnight.*

Perfect Timing

How did *The Da Vinci Code* defy the critics to become a '60-million-copies-in-44-languages' publishers' dream, with a 227 million dollar-grossing movie to match, for which Brown received 6 million dollars for the rights alone? And why did Brown's two previous books not achieve the same success given that it is clear he has, in his Destiny Code, the potential to be a successful author? For that answer, we must look at the dynamic element of his BaZi, the Luck Pillars.

The Luck Pillars represent the dynamic aspect of a person's BaZi. They unlock the potential of the BaZi during certain periods, when the elements interact in a particular manner to create certain outcomes, but are also capable of creating obstacles. Brown's Day Master is weak and his chart is hot, so the Useful God and Favourable element for his chart is Water, specifically Gui Water or Yin Water.

Brown's previous Luck Pillar, during the years of 1988-1997, creates an unfavourable combination in his chart between the You 酉 (Rooster) in his chart and the Chen 辰 (Dragon). This combination removes the Chen 辰 (Dragon), thus removing the roots of the Jia Wood. During this time period, his Direct Resource is combined away, so there is no one to help him out in his endeavours. It also compromises the quality of his Eating God star, taking away opportunities for him.

All of this changes in 1998, when Brown enters the Xu 戌 (Dog) pillar of his Luck Pillars. It was in this year that his first mystery book, *Digital Fortress*, was released, but even then it didn't sell too well at the time. A humour book and *Angels and Demons* followed. Neither sold more than 10,000 copies at the time, according to Wikipedia. Then came *The Da Vinci Code* in 2003 and within weeks it was on the New York Times Bestseller list. What happened?

The Xu 戌 (Dog) Luck Pillar represents a good pillar for Brown because the Dog and Dragon clash, releasing Gui or Yin Water. This is an extremely favourable element for Brown's chart because he is a weak Ren Water and needs the Rob Wealth star to strengthen him. But even within a favourable Luck Pillar, good luck does not come overnight. It doesn't work like instant noodles!

In 2003, Gui Water appears in the Stem of the year, so Brown's most needed and most useful element appears that year. It not only strengthens the Day Master, but nourishes the Jia Wood or Eating God star. Suddenly, the Qi in the chart is flowing. Furthermore, the Dog luck pillar creates a powerful 3 Harmony combination of Yin Wu Xu, which produces Fire, his Wealth element. Wealth is extremely powerful but now the self is strong, so he can 'take' or handle the wealth.

Will the Luck Hold?

In 2008, Brown will change Luck Pillars and enter Hai 亥 (Pig) Luck. This period will signal intensifying competition and his rivals will prove to be formidable. Furthermore the Hai 亥 (Pig) combines with the Yin 寅 (Tiger) and the Wu 午 (Horse), weakening his Wealth Luck. Thus, whilst the Hai 亥 (Pig) remains a favourable Pillar generally, because it contains Water he will probably not make much money during that Luck Pillar.

But then with 250 million in the bank, arguably that is the least of his concerns!

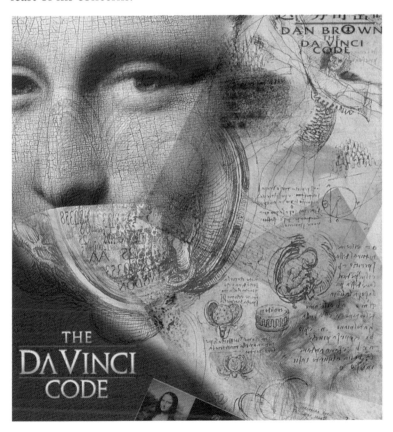

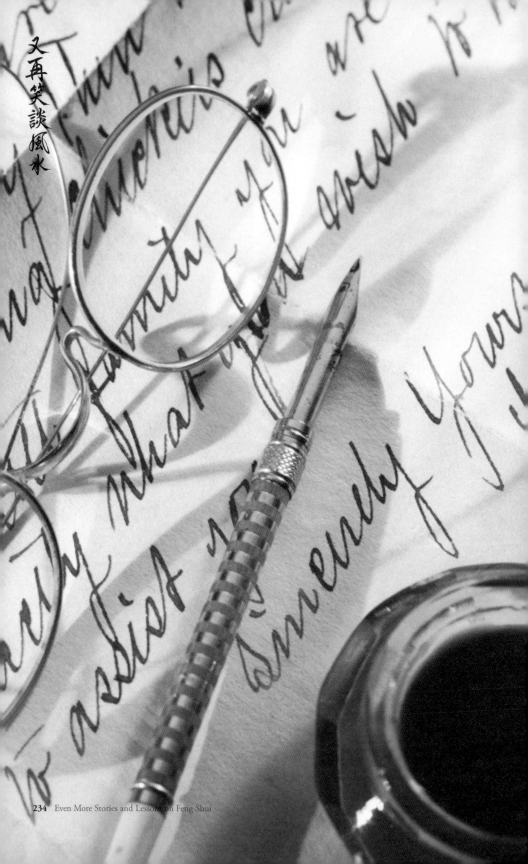

又再笑談風水

The Top Unwanted Five of Feng Shui

Most people buy homes to provide a roof over their heads, or as a form of investment. In Feng Shui, the approach will vary slightly depending on whether you are looking to buy the property as an investment or as a home. But some of the basic rules remain applicable, irrespective of whether you're an investor or home owner. I'll share with you five features you DON'T want to see in a house, regardless of whether you are buying to invest or to occupy. And these are features that anyone, irrespective of their Feng Shui background, can spot easily.

These five tips will focus on what features you should avoid having in a house. Now, I'm sure you're thinking: "Surely it can be fixed?" Fixing is always secondary, because what is the point in spending money to better something that is bad, when you can spend the money improving something that is already good? With Feng Shui, we like to start from a positive position and improve it further, rather than begin from a negative position and then spend money to get it to an 'average' place. So what constitutes the not-so-fabulous Feng Shui Top Five to avoid? Check them out below – I've included photos to help you understand exactly what these negative five features look like in a property.

The Doorway to 'No Thanks'

The Main Door of a house is also known as the Qi Mouth of the property. It is through the Main Door that the Qi from the environment flows in. If the Main Door effectively and literally 'sucks,' then you don't even need to waste time looking at the rest of the house, because it can't be that good. In Feng Shui,

Some exmaples of bad Main Doors.

we assess the main door using a Formula-based assessment (based on the direction of the Main Door) and Forms-based assessments. Forms are the easiest way to check out the Feng Shui affecting the Main Door, especially for laypersons.

So what are the signs of a bad Main Door? Well, a lamp post, a tree or an electrical pole smack in the middle of the Main Door? Forget it. Tilted Main Doors are a definite no-no as these not only cause Sha Qi problems but also can result in the Main Door facing a pillar. Avoid houses with beams running across the Main Door (both inside and outside). If you do venture in and discover the Main Door is located below the toilet of the Master Bedroom or any bedroom, this is again not conducive to Qi flow and should be avoided.

Nothing should block Main Doors and entrances.

Kitchen Confidential

Health aspects of a house are usually dictated or largely influenced by the Kitchen, specifically the positioning or location of the stove. This is because the kitchen is where we cook food, and food directly impacts on the health of the residents of a property. If the Qi in the kitchen is bad, the quality of health of the residents deteriorates. You want to avoid a kitchen that is located in the center of the house, as this disrupts the TaiJi (heart) of the house. You also want to avoid a house with a kitchen where the only place to locate the stove is in the center (sometimes called an Island Stove).

Stoves should not be in the center of kitchens

If It Looks Like a Drain...

Open drains directly in front of the house are known as Feet-Cutting Sha - these cause Sha Qi and can actually bring about detrimental effects to the occupants of a property, especially when it comes to money matters.

Don't buy into the claims of the real estate agent or owner telling you that the drain is a Water Dragon that will create tremendous wealth. For a Water Dragon to be a real Water Dragon, it must be natural, meaning that it exists in the environment in a natural water formation. So when you see a drain that runs right around the house, remember that old saying: if it looks like a drain, and it functions like a drain – it's a DRAIN.

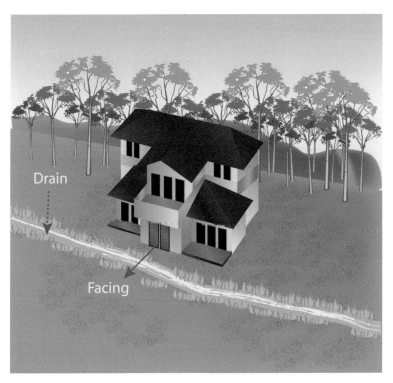

Open drain in front of houses cause Sha Qi.

又再笑談風水

Beware the Menacing Road

Most house owners look at roads near the property to see if it will be noisy or perhaps even encourage illegal midnight car races. When it comes to Feng Shui, what you have to look out for are the curves on the road. You don't want to select a property where the road curves into the house like a blade. If possible, you also don't want alleys, narrow or wide, opposite the property. A very narrow alley can cause either a Pulling Nose Qi problem or a Sky Crack Sha problem (depending on the type of alley) and this is usually very, very hard to fix. The best thing to do is avoid it altogether.

Road curving into the house like a blade.

Bedroom Boo-Boos

Generally, irregular-shaped bedrooms should be avoided in any house as it means the Qi in the room is not stable. This usually results in disrupted sleep. The best kind of bedroom is a square-shaped room. You also do not want sloping ceilings or low ceilings as this suppresses the Qi, resulting again in disrupted or poor-quality sleep.

These are of course just a few key negative Feng Shui features for which you should be on the lookout when it comes to a property. Bear in mind that this only scratches the surface of Feng Shui basics; there is plenty more to consider when it comes to a proper, thorough implementation of Feng Shui for your place of residence. However, you can consider this 'The Big Five' of Feng Shui home no-no's. Knowing these fundamentals can at least put your worries to rest when you buy or rent a home for yourself because at least you know you've got the major taboo aspects covered. You may, quite literally, 'rest easy!'

Avoid irregular-shaped bedrooms because of unstable Qi.

又再笑談風水

No Flying Broomsticks in Feng Shui

Many people equate Feng Shui consultants with miracle-making abilities. Clients sometimes think that Feng Shui consultants can wave a magic wand, apply a formula and make all their problems disappear, or turn them into millionaires when they follow certain water formulas. Feng Shui does not work like that. It is not magic. Feng Shui consultants are not graduates of Hogwarts!

Let's go back to the basics. Feng Shui is about tapping and making use of the correct Qi in the environment, thus maximising the potential of the environment around your property to improve the quality of your life. There are many positive improvements that Feng Shui can bring to a person's life but one has to be cautioned that there are also limitations to what Feng Shui can do, particularly if the role played by Feng Shui is not understood correctly.

When the Qi in the environment is working for you, you feel better, you are more energized, motivated, and alert, and you are able to respond to opportunities better. This contributes to your ability to perform better at work and enjoy positive relationships with those around you. When you are happy and relaxed, you are able to pursue your goals with a clear mind. Often, wealth and increased prosperity or affluence is an outcome of this positive state of affairs.

But having the best Feng Shui in the world is of no benefit if the person does not take any action. Sometimes, people have the misconception that once they utilise Feng Shui, there's no need to lift a finger – the formula (or if you are into New Age Feng Shui, the trinket, amulet or figurine) will do everything for you. As much as I don't want to shatter anyone's illusions, Feng Shui cannot make money or miracles from nothing. Old-fashioned hard work is also required.

In Feng Shui, there are techniques and systems that can be used to produce quick results or bring about results that are more swiftly noticeable. For example, using Water formulas often brings about faster results than using Mountain formulas. But of course, Water also does not bring about lasting results. For that, you need to use Mountains. Similarly, the Eight Mansions system produces more steady and gradual results and is suitable for long-term outcomes whilst the Flying Stars system produces quicker, short-term outcomes. But no matter what system is used, not taking action is simply a zero-sum gain. So I'm going to share with you why action matters more than most people realize when it comes to matters of Feng Shui.

The Philosophy of the Cosmic Trinity

One of the core concepts of Chinese Metaphysics is the theory of the Cosmic Trinity. The Cosmic Trinity refers to the three factors that influence our lives: Heaven, Earth and Man. Each of these three factors exerts an equal amount of influence on us, which if you are into percentages, is around 33.33%.

Heaven refers to a person's Destiny and the life path that is laid out for a person at the time of his birth, as influenced by the stars, elements and Qi present in the solar system at the time of the person's birth. Chinese Astrology, either through BaZi or Purple Star Astrology, is how consultants decipher a person's Destiny.

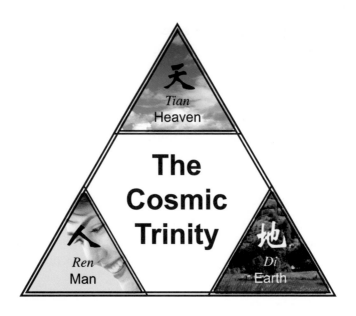

Heaven 天 *Tian*	The talents that you are born with, potentials and the capacity to make the most of your potential. Your family background, health condition and where you are born is also determined by Heaven Luck.
Man 人 *Ren*	The actions that you take to capitalize upon your potential and also opportunities that may present themselves. Your education, perseverance, beliefs and principle also form the basis of your Man Luck.
Earth 地 *Di*	The area in which you reside. This is what is known as Feng Shui. Your external environment, where you work and where your home is located all plays a role in your Earth Luck.

Earth refers to the environment in which a person lives in or works in. It is this particular aspect of the Cosmic Trinity that Feng Shui looks to address and improve.

Finally, Man refers to the actions and choices that a person makes in life – his or her beliefs, education, aspirations and virtues.

SUPERIOR DESTINY
EXCELLENT FENG SHUI
ABILITY AND WISDOM
RIGHT CHOICE
RIGHT ACTION

All of the above three factors are inter-related. They do not function in isolation. For example, in an ideal situation, a person would have good Heaven Luck (a superior Destiny), good Earth Luck (excellent Feng Shui) and good Man Luck (the ability and wisdom to make the right choice and take the right action). When all three factors operate in tandem, everything is smooth.

However, when there is a problem with any one of these factors, then it also impacts on the other components. For example, if a person is not going through favourable Heaven luck, according to his BaZi (Eight Characters or Destiny chart), then the chances of that person being able to find a good house or live in a place with favourable Feng Shui (i.e. the Earth Luck component) is reduced. Accordingly, he has to rely on the action he takes or the choices he makes (i.e. the Man Luck component) to overcome any obstacles or problems he is facing.

又再笑談風水

Likewise, if a person is not destined to be a millionaire, then from a wealth perspective that person starts out at a disadvantage. In these instances, Feng Shui can help bring about some improvement but the rest has to be old-fashioned hard work and financial prudence – making the right choices and taking the right action.

Many clients and students of Feng Shui find it difficult to understand this concept because they often try to reason or understand how it all works together. The Cosmic Trinity is really a metaphysical chicken and egg scenario – we could go on and on about which comes first, which matters more, and which is of higher priority. I think it's much more important for people to appreciate the concept and understand that the Cosmic Trinity illustrates the point that taking action, and especially taking the right action at the right time, is just as important as having the right Feng Shui.

Doing the Right Thing, At the Right Time

BaZi is a good example of how action is just as important as knowing what destiny has in store for a person. When a client comes for a BaZi analysis consultation, we help our clients understand their life path, their talents and abilities, and guide them on how they could capitalise on their best years and lie low during the difficult years. However, I always emphasise to clients that it is one thing to know your personal potential and what Destiny has in store for you, but it is another thing to actually achieve it. For that, a person needs to take action and make the right choices.

For example, let's say that someone has great potential to be a writer or perhaps a music star. If this person simply sits at home and does nothing but watch television and idle his time away, then his potential is not achieved because he did not take any action and thus, did not put himself in a position to maximise his talent and potential. Knowing your abilities and potential is one thing. But not doing anything means you are not going to achieve the greatness you were destined to achieve.

So what does this all mean when it comes to Feng Shui? Firstly, my goal in this article is to enable my readers to understand and appreciate why Feng Shui is not a miracle practice, and why it is not magic. It is simply because it is just one of the components of the Cosmic Trinity.

Secondly, it is important that people appreciate the limitations of Feng Shui. Yes, I have talked about how Feng Shui, when properly utilised, can create Emperors and build empires. But all this does not happen because of Feng Shui alone. There is a Heaven component to it and a Man aspect to it as well. Often, it is hard for Feng Shui enthusiasts to understand why after paying a considerable amount of money and spending hours on fine-tuning their house, they are still not millionaires or getting what they wanted to achieve. The Cosmic Trinity offers the answer to that question.

Thirdly, it is important that anyone who intends to seek the advice of a Feng Shui consultant knows that Destiny analysis

is an important component in the practice of Feng Shui. Through the use of BaZi 八字 (also known as Eight Characters or Four Pillars of Destiny) or Zi Wei Dou Shu 紫微斗數 (Purple Star Astrology), Destiny Analysis provides the means to achieve a diagnosis of a person's challenges or problems in life. Feng Shui is only the prescription. Some Feng Shui practitioners make recommendations or suggest Feng Shui remedies without carrying out a personal destiny analysis of their clients. When Feng Shui remedies are suggested without an analysis of a person's Destiny through BaZi or Zi Wei, it is like giving a 'cure' or a prescription without a proper diagnosis, and it is unlikely that the remedies will be effective.

It is possible that some Feng Shui practitioners do not like to talk about limitations. Perhaps it may be because shattering people's dreams is difficult and unpleasant. Or maybe it is easier for them to give hope to their clients rather than to tell them that the only way for them to be wealthy or successful in this lifetime is to **work hard!** And perhaps, it doesn't sound like what most people want to hear in this age and era of instant gratification. But if Feng Shui is to gain recognition as a credible profession, then it is important for people to know that Feng Shui has its own inherent limitations because Feng Shui consultants are not in the business of creating miracles. It is important for people to understand this. For starters, it will certainly go a long way towards preventing people from being

taken for a ride when it comes to Feng Shui because they can now understand the context in which Feng Shui is utilised, and be fully knowledgeable on what it can and cannot do.

This is not to say that Feng Shui is of zero help either. If your Destiny is not so favourable or advantaged, with hard work and focus on the person's part, plus a little extra push from Feng Shui, achieving your goals and dreams in life is not impossible. You may not get to your aim as quickly and speedily as a person with a better Destiny, but you could still get there eventually. And isn't that, after all, the most important thing?

又再笑談風水

又再笑談風水

Dear Feng Shui Master

I frequently write for newspapers and publications, and ever since I began doing it my email inbox has always been inundated with questions from readers. Some people are simply curious to know more about Feng Shui in general, others are seeking specific answers to their Feng Shui queries, and many more are just looking for some comfort or confirmation about some superstitions, old wives' tales, and myths.

So I thought that for a change I should open up my mailbag and share with you some of the more common (and interesting) queries I've received and the answers to these queries. Some of these questions may be a bit technical, while others are more straightforward. But these share a common element as they represent, for the most part, general questions that people usually think or wonder about when it comes to the subject of Feng Shui.

I employed the services of a Feng Shui Master (a friend of mine) when we shifted to our new house in June last year. According to her, our house is Northeast facing (main door facing NE) and is an 'Earth' house. She had told us not to use colours like red, blue, purple for our house but to use colours like beige, white, brown and light yellow. However, in the recent yearly review which we had asked her to do for the house, she told us we cannot use green. I had already bought green material for my curtain and sofa set since she had not mentioned not to use green the first time. Now she says green, which is a 'Wood' colour, will destroy the Earth house. I still remember her saying that colours will only affect 10% of Feng Shui but when I asked her if it was okay if I went ahead to have green sofa set and curtain, she said definitely not.

I am now very confused. I do not want to get rid of the green materials which I had spent quite a lot of money on, but on the other hand, I'm afraid it will be bad Feng Shui. There are other things which she has said that seems contradictory but since she is a friend, it is difficult for us to question her too much. Is it true that I cannot use the green materials? Can you please let me know what the good and bad colours for the house are? Is it true that I can put certain colors only for certain years?

In the basic study of Feng Shui, a building may be of a certain element, based on its general shape. For example, a building with a sharp pointy roof is a Fire form. Round-shaped or designed buildings are of Metal element. In Eight Mansions Feng Shui, the element of a house is based on the Sitting direction of the house. However, the element of your house really does not impact on your personal choices when it comes to interior decoration.

Your Feng Shui consultant friend seems to have based her interior design recommendations on New Age Feng Shui rather than Classical Feng Shui. The elemental quality of a building also does not dictate your interior design choices. It simply tells us what the building is better suited for, from a functionality point-of-view. Just because you have a Fire form house, does not mean you cannot have blue sofas or blue curtains based on the over-simplified notion that 'Water and Fire Clash.' If you like your green curtains and green sofa, keep them. The operative word here is 'like.' Colours, quite frankly, have nothing very much to do with Feng Shui and their effect or impact is largely psychological.

Defining your Feng Shui by colours, based on elemental considerations, would seem highly illogical and impractical because this means you've got to repaint your house and change all your furniture every year since the elemental energies keep changing. Classical Feng Shui doesn't require anything of this sort (and anyway, in the ancient days of the Tang Dynasty, most houses looked the same and had the same colours!). There are no good colours or bad colours, only colours you like, and colours you don't like!

We bought a house recently. Is there any special date selection for moving in?

Date selection is important if we want to maximize the benefits and enjoy the long-lasting effects of good Feng Shui. For an important activity like house moving, selection of a suitable date is highly recommended.

The purpose of date selection is to do the right thing at the right time. Right time in this case means we should choose a specific date where energies of the day are in tandem with the Qi pattern that we are trying to activate, and a specific time when the positive energies in our surrounding are at its optimal level for the action or activity to be initiated.

The Tong Shu or Chinese Almanac, which has been a common household item for most Chinese families for the last few hundred years, contains some generic suitable dates for moving into a new house. However, these are meant for general use only.

Date Selection is a specialized field of study in itself, with numerous methodologies available for selecting suitable dates such as the Dong Gong Method, Xuan Kong Da Gua, Qi Men, Shen Sha and Tian Xing Method, to name just a few. A really good date for any activity (be it moving house, or opening a new business) is a date personalised to the person or persons in question who are involved in the activity. This is done by matching the date to the BaZi (or Destiny Code) of the people involved.

I own a black-coloured car but met with 2 accidents in 8 months. I was born in the year of the Dragon, and am now aged 31. I feel that the colour black is not suitable for me and I have decided to change the paint colour this weekend. Please advise me on which colour is more suitable for me.

This reminds me of a recent article my student in England sent to me about how you can Feng Shui your car and avoid accidents, thus reducing your insurance payments! Unlike a house, your car does not have a fixed Facing Direction or a location. You do not sleep or live in your car. Accordingly, your car has no Feng Shui effect on you. So, it's not because of the 'Feng Shui of the car' that you have experienced accidents. Neither has the colour of your car (nor its number plate) nor the type of car had anything to do with the number of accidents you have encountered. Paint your car whatever colour YOU LIKE. As for the issue of accidents, it's more likely that there's a problem in your BaZi or maybe it's your driving that is causing the problem, rather than your car!

I would like to know if it is not good for a couple who is born in the same year to be together? My boyfriend and I were born in the Dragon year and we are always being told that we can't be together! They said it's "zhong" (clash). Is it true?

In the study of BaZi, there are six Earthly Branches that are in a Clash relationship with each other. The Dragon is in a Clash relationship with the Dog - so to first answer the question, there is no such thing as a Dragon-Dragon Clash.

The Clash relationships in the study of BaZi have led to some creative interpretations, extending to the conclusion that individuals should not date or marry, or engage in joint-ventures or partnerships with people whose year Branch clashes with their year Branch. For example, a person born in the year of the Pig should not partner or marry a person born in the year of the Snake. This is simply not quite correct!

Compatibility between individuals is not determined by the Year Branch alone – instead, it is done through the comparison of the entire BaZi (or Destiny Codes) of both individuals. Anyway, surely it's illogical to have to break up a relationship with someone or exclude dating somebody or

avoid doing business with someone just because they happen to be of an Animal sign that clashes with our own? We have to look at the complete BaZi charts of the individuals in order to reach a more accurate conclusion.

Is it true that with your exact date and time of birth, black magic can be performed on you? If it's true, isn't it dangerous to give away such information?

BaZi consultants or Destiny Analysts are not in the business of hexing or performing black magic. This fear, unfortunately, stems from the old days when there were quite a number of Feng Shui masters doubling up as spiritual masters. Today, most Feng Shui and BaZi consultants are strictly masters of their own field, leaving out spiritual practices, including ghost-busting activities, which are, in the first place, not a part of classical Feng Shui or Chinese astrology.

The trend among Feng Shui and BaZi consultants today is already increasingly shifting back towards pure Classical Feng Shui and Chinese astrology which is strictly focused on the study of natural environment (i.e. capacity of earth energy) and destiny analysis (capacity of man). Besides, most Feng Shui and BaZi consultants today, by virtue of modern day expectations, are highly professional in their approach. Information about birth details or house details is normally treated in a highly confidential manner. So there's no 'danger,' so to speak.

Of course, despite what have been discussed, you may be one of those who are still concerned and nervous about giving away such information. There is in fact a way to overcome this. Many of you may not be aware that each Chinese Hour is actually two Western Hours – as in Dragon Hour (7 am to 9 am) or Rooster Hour (5 pm to 7 pm). So if you want to have some piece of mind when engaging the services of a Feng Shui and BaZi consultant, just tell the consultant your time of birth according to the Chinese Hour!

My company intends to buy a new set of premises, but we have 5 directors. If I want to choose the facing direction based on an individual's Gua number, which director's Gua number should I follow?

This is a common question when it comes to Feng Shui for business premises. Using the personal Gua of individual directors to find new business premises is okay for a small company or a sole proprietorship, but this doesn't quite work for large corporations or companies where there are many directors who are not all from the same personal Gua group - in other words, some directors may belong to the East Group, and some to West Group. In Classical Feng Shui, the approach is not to use the directors' personal Gua alone to find the right premises, but rather, to locate the office or purchase an office in an area with good environmental forms first so that the quality of Qi is good and supports that type of business. Next, a classical Feng Shui consultant will check the House Gua, which I have written about in the past. Once the House Gua is determined, the individual directors will be placed in the appropriate sectors of the building. Additional fine-tuning will then be done using the Personal Gua of the directors and Xuan Kong Flying Stars or Da Gua and also opening the Main Door in a good sector.

If the main entrance of the building of my apartment faces Southeast and my unit main door faces East - how do I get the House Gua? Based on Southeast or East?

When it comes to apartments, you will need to determine the Facing and Sitting direction of the whole apartment block in order to accurately determine the property's House Gua. It's not enough to simply know the Facing Direction of your own apartment unit's Main Entrance as this may not always represent the facing direction of the whole apartment block.

About Joey Yap

Joey Yap is the Founder and Master Trainer of the Mastery Academy of Chinese Metaphysics, a global organisation devoted to the worldwide teaching of Feng Shui, BaZi, Mian Xiang, Yi Jing and other Chinese Metaphysics subjects. Joey is also the Chief Consultant of Yap Global Consulting, an international Feng Shui and Chinese Astrology consulting firm offering audit and consultation services to corporations and individuals all over the world.

Joey received his formal education in Malaysia and Australia. He has combined the best of Eastern learning and Western education systems in the teaching methodology practiced at the Academy. Students of the Mastery Academy study traditional syllabuses of Chinese Metaphysics but through Western-style modular programs that are structured and systematic, enabling individuals to easily and quickly learn, grasp and master complex Chinese Metaphysics subjects like Feng Shui and BaZi. These unique structured learning systems are also utilized by Mastery Academy instructors all over the world to teach BaZi and Feng Shui.

The Mastery Academy is also the first international educational organisation to fully utilize the benefits of the Internet to promote continuous education, encourage peer-to-peer learning, enable mentoring and distance learning. Students interact with each other live, and continue to learn and improve their knowledge.

Despite his busy schedule, Joey continues to write for the Mastery Journal, a monthly eZine on Feng Shui and Astrology devoted for world-wide readers and the production of the world's first bilingual *Ten Thousand Year Calendar*. He is also the best selling author of *Stories and Lessons on Feng Shui, Mian Xiang- Discover Face Reading, Tong Shu Diary, BaZi - The Destiny Code, BaZi - The Destiny Code Revealed, Feng Shui for Homebuyers-Interior, Feng Shui for Homebuyers-Exterior* and the *Mini Feng Shui Compass*. Besides being a regular guest of various radio and TV talk shows, Joey is also a regular columnist for a national newspaper and various magazines in Malaysia. In fact, he hosted his own *TV series, Discover Feng Shui with Joey Yap*, on Malaysia's 8TV channel in 2005; a popular program that focused on heightening awareness of Feng Shui and Chinese Metaphysics.

A firm believer in innovation being the way forward, Joey recently released the BaZi Ming Pan 2.0 software, which allows users to generate configurable, detailed BaZi charts.

Author's personal website: www.joeyyap.com | www.fengshuilogy.com
Academy website: www.masteryacademy.com | www.masteryjournal.com |
www.maelearning.com

EDUCATION
The Mastery Academy of Chinese Metaphysics:
the first choice for practitioners and aspiring students of the
art and science of Chinese Classical Feng Shui and Astrology.

For thousands of years, Eastern knowledge has been passed from one generation to another through the system of discipleship. A venerated master would accept suitable individuals at a young age as his disciples, and informally through the years, pass on his knowledge and skills to them. His disciples in turn, would take on their own disciples, as a means to perpetuate knowledge or skills.

This system served the purpose of restricting the transfer of knowledge to only worthy honourable individuals and ensuring that outsiders or Westerners would not have access to thousands of years of Eastern knowledge, learning and research.

However, the disciple system has also resulted in Chinese Metaphysics and Classical Studies lacking systematic teaching methods. Knowledge garnered over the years has not been accumulated in a concise, systematic manner, but scattered amongst practitioners, each practicing his/her knowledge, art and science, in isolation.

The disciple system, out of place in today's modern world, endangers the advancement of these classical fields that continue to have great relevance and application today.

At the Mastery Academy of Chinese Metaphysics, our Mission is to bring Eastern Classical knowledge in the fields of metaphysics, Feng Shui and Astrology sciences and the arts to the world. These Classical teachings and knowledge, previously shrouded in secrecy and passed on only through the discipleship system, are adapted into structured learning, which can easily be understood, learnt and mastered. Through modern learning methods, these renowned ancient arts, sciences and practices can be perpetuated while facilitating more extensive application and understanding of these classical subjects.

The Mastery Academy espouses an educational philosophy that draws from the best of the East and West. It is the world's premier educational institution for the study of Chinese Metaphysics Studies offering a wide range and variety of courses, ensuring that students have the opportunity to pursue their preferred field of study and enabling existing practitioners and professionals to gain cross-disciplinary knowledge that complements their current field of practice.

Courses at the Mastery Academy have been carefully designed to ensure a comprehensive yet compact syllabus. The modular nature of the courses enables students to immediately begin to put their knowledge into practice while pursuing continued study of their field and complementary fields. Students thus have the benefit of developing and gaining practical experience in tandem with the expansion and advancement of their theoretical knowledge.

Students can also choose from a variety of study options, from a distance learning program, the Homestudy Series, that enables study at one's own pace or intensive foundation courses and compact lecture-based courses, held in various cities around the world by Joey Yap or our licensed instructors. The Mastery Academy's faculty and make-up is international in nature, thus ensuring that prospective students can attend courses at destinations nearest to their country of origin or with a licensed Mastery Academy instructor in their home country.

The Mastery Academy provides 24x7 support to students through its Online Community, with a variety of tools, documents, forums and e-learning materials to help students stay at the forefront of research in their fields and gain invaluable assistance from peers and mentoring from their instructors.

TM

MASTERY ACADEMY
OF CHINESE METAPHYSICS

www.masteryacademy.com

MALAYSIA
19-3, The Boulevard
Mid Valley City
59200 Kuala Lumpur, Malaysia
Tel   : +603-2284 8080
Fax   : +603-2284 1218
Email : info@masteryacademy.com

SINGAPORE
14, Robinson Road # 13-00
Far East Finance Building
Singapore 048545
Tel   : +65-6722 8775
Fax   : +65-3125 7131
Email : singapore@masteryacademy.com

AUSTRALIA
Unit 3 / 61 Belmont Avenue,
Belmont WA 6104.
Australia.
Tel   : +618-9467 3626
Fax   : +618-9479 3388
Email : australia@masteryacademy.com

Represented in:
Australia, Austria, Brazil, Canada, China, Cyprus, France, Germany, Greece, Hungary, India, Japan, Indonesia, Italy, Malaysia, Mexico, Netherlands, New Zealand, Philippines, Russian Federation, Poland, Singapore, South Africa, Switzerland, Turkey, U.S.A., Ukraine, United Kingdom

Introducing...
The Mastery Academy's E-Learning Center!

The Mastery Academy's goal has always been to share authentic knowledge of Chinese Metaphysics with the whole world.

Nevertheless, we do recognize that distance, time, and hotel and traveling costs – amongst many other factors – could actually hinder people from enrolling for a classroom-based course. But with the advent and amazing advance of IT today, NOT any more!

With this in mind, we have invested heavily in IT, to conceive what is probably the first and only E-Learning Center in the world today that offers a full range of studies in the field of Chinese Metaphysics.

Convenient   Study from Your   Easy Enrollment
Own Home

The Mastery Academy's E-Learning Center

Now, armed with your trusty computer or laptop, and Internet access, knowledge of classical Feng Shui, BaZi (Destiny Analysis) and Mian Xiang (Face Reading) are but a literal click away!

Study at your own pace, and interact with your Instructor and fellow students worldwide, from anywhere in the world. With our E-Learning Center, knowledge of Chinese Metaphysics is brought DIRECTLY to you in all its clarity – topic-by-topic, and lesson-by-lesson; with illustrated presentations and comprehensive notes expediting your learning curve!

Your education journey through our E-Learning Center may be done via any of the following approaches:

1. Online Courses

There are 3 Programs available: our Online Feng Shui Program, Online BaZi Program, and Online Mian Xiang Program. Each Program consists of several Levels, with each Level consisting of many Lessons in turn. Each Lesson contains a pre-recorded video session on the topic at hand, accompanied by presentation-slides and graphics as well as downloadable tutorial notes that you can print and file for future reference.

Video Lecture | Presentation Slide | Downloadable Notes

2. MA Live!

MA Live!, as its name implies, enables LIVE broadcasts of Joey Yap's courses and seminars – right to your computer screen. Students will not only get to see and hear Joey talk on real-time `live', but also participate and more importantly, TALK to Joey via the MA Live! interface. All the benefits of a live class, minus the hassle of actually having to attend one!

How It Works

Our Live Classes   You at Home

3. Video-On-Demand (VOD)

Get immediate streaming-downloads of the Mastery Academy's wide range of educational DVDs, right on your computer screen. No more shipping costs and waiting time to be incurred!

Instant VOD Online

Choose From Our list of Available VODs!   Click "Play" on Your PC

Welcome to **www.maelearning.com**; the web portal of our E-Learning Center, and YOUR virtual gateway to Chinese Metaphysics!

Mastery Academy around the world

United States
Canada
Mexico
Brazil

United Kingdom
Switzerland
Netherlands
France
Italy
Cyprus
Austria
Poland
Germany
Hungary
Greece
Turkey
Russian Federation
Ukraine

South Africa

China
Japan
India
Philippines
Kuala Lumpur
Malaysia
Indonesia
Singapore
Australia
New Zealand

YAP GLOBAL CONSULTING

Joey Yap & Yap Global Consulting

Headed by Joey Yap, Yap Global Consulting (YGC) is a leading international consulting firm specializing in Feng Shui, Mian Xiang (Face Reading) and BaZi (Destiny Analysis) consulting services worldwide. Joey - an internationally renowned Master Trainer, Consultant, Speaker and best-selling Author - has dedicated his life to the art and science of Chinese Metaphysics.

YGC has its main offices in Kuala Lumpur and Australia, and draws upon its diverse reservoir of strength from a group of dedicated and experienced consultants based in more than 30 countries, worldwide.

As the pioneer in blending established, classical Chinese Metaphysics techniques with the latest approach in consultation practices, YGC has built its reputation on the principles of professionalism and only the highest standards of service. This allows us to retain the cutting edge in delivering Feng Shui and Destiny consultation services to both corporate and personal clients, in a simple and direct manner, without compromising on quality.

Across Industries: Our Portfolio of Clients

Our diverse portfolio of both corporate and individual clients from all around the world bears testimony to our experience and capabilities.

Virtually every industry imaginable has benefited from our services - ranging from academic and financial institutions, real-estate developers and multinational corporations, to those in the leisure and tourism industry. Our services are also engaged by professionals, prominent business personalities, celebrities, high-profile politicians and people from all walks of life.

YAP GLOBAL CONSULTING

Name (Mr./Mrs./Ms.):

Contact Details

Tel: _____ Fax: _____

Mobile : _____

E-mail: _____

What Type of Consultation Are You Interested In?
☐ Feng Shui   ☐ BaZi   ☐ Date Selection   ☐ Yi Jing

Please tick if applicable:

☐ Are you a Property Developer looking to engage Yap Global Consulting?

☐ Are you a Property Investor looking for tailor-made packages to suit your investment requirements?

Please attach your name card here.

Thank you for completing this form.
Please fax it back to us at:

Singapore	Australia	Malaysia & the rest of the world
Fax: +65-3125 7131	Fax: +618-9479 3388	Fax: +603-2284 2213
Tel : +65-6722 8775	Tel : +618-9467 3626	Tel : +603-2284 1213

---

w w w . j o e y y a p . c o m

Feng Shui Consultations

For Residential Properties
- Initial Land/Property Assessment
- Residential Feng Shui Consultations
- Residential Land Selection
- End-to-End Residential Consultation

For Commercial Properties
- Initial Land/Property Assessment
- Commercial Feng Shui Consultations
- Commercial Land Selection
- End-to-End Commercial Consultation

For Property Developers
- End-to-End Consultation
- Post-Consultation Advisory Services
- Panel Feng Shui Consultant

For Property Investors
- Your Personal Feng Shui Consultant
- Tailor-Made Packages

For Memorial Parks & Burial Sites
- Yin House Feng Shui

BaZi Consultations

Personal Destiny Analysis
- Personal Destiny Analysis for Individuals
- Children's BaZi Analysis
- Family BaZi Analysis

Strategic Analysis for Corporate Organizations
- Corporate BaZi Consultations
- BaZi Analysis for Human Resource Management

Entrepreneurs & Business Owners
- BaZi Analysis for Entrepreneurs

Career Pursuits
- BaZi Career Analysis

Relationships
- Marriage and Compatibility Analysis
- Partnership Analysis

For Everyone
- Annual BaZi Forecast
- Your Personal BaZi Coach

Date Selection Consultations

- **Marriage Date Selection**
- **Caesarean Birth Date Selection**
- **House-Moving Date Selection**
- **Renovation & Groundbreaking Dates**

- **Signing of Contracts**
- **Official Openings**
- **Product Launches**

Yi Jing Assessment

A Time-Tested, Accurate Science

- With a history predating 4 millennia, the Yi Jing - or Classic of Change - is one of the oldest Chinese texts surviving today. Its purpose as an oracle, in predicting the outcome of things, is based on the variables of Time, Space and Specific Events.

- A Yi Jing Assessment provides specific answers to any specific questions you may have about a specific event or endeavor. This is something that a Destiny Analysis would not be able to give you.

Basically, what a Yi Jing Assessment does is focus on only ONE aspect or item at a particular point in your life, and give you a calculated prediction of the details that will follow suit, if you undertake a particular action. It gives you an insight into a situation, and what course of action to take in order to arrive at a satisfactory outcome at the end of the day.

Please Contact YGC for a personalized Yi Jing Assessment!

INVITING US TO YOUR CORPORATE EVENTS

Many reputable organizations and institutions have worked closely with YGC to build a synergistic business relationship by engaging our team of consultants, led by Joey Yap, as speakers at their corporate events. Our seminars and short talks are always packed with audiences consisting of clients and associates of multinational and public-listed companies as well as key stakeholders of financial institutions.

We tailor our seminars and talks to suit the anticipated or pertinent group of audience. Be it a department, subsidiary, your clients or even the entire corporation, we aim to fit your requirements in delivering the intended message(s).

Tel: +603-2284 1213   Email: consultation@joeyyap.com

Latest DVDs Release by Joey Yap
Feng Shui for Homebuyers DVD Series

Best-selling Author, and international Master Trainer and Consultant Joey Yap reveals in these DVDs the significant Feng Shui features that every homebuyer should know when evaluating a property.

Joey will guide you on how to customise your home to maximise the Feng Shui potential of your property and gain the full benefit of improving your health, wealth and love life using the 9 Palace Grid. He will show you how to go about applying the classical applications of the Life Gua and House Gua techniques to get attuned to your Sheng Qi (positive energies).

In these DVDs, you will also learn how to identify properties with good Feng Shui features that will help you promote a fulfilling life and achieve your full potential. Discover how to avoid properties with negative Feng Shui that can bring about detrimental effects to your health, wealth and relationships.

Joey will also elaborate on how to fix the various aspects of your home that may have an impact on the Feng Shui of your property and give pointers on how to tap into the positive energies to support your goals.

Discover Feng Shui with Joey Yap (TV Series)

Discover Feng Shui with Joey Yap: Set of 4 DVDs

Informative and entertaining, classical Feng Shui comes alive in *Discover Feng Shui with Joey Yap!*

Dying to know how you can use Feng Shui to improve your house or office, but simply too busy attend for formal classes?

You have the questions. Now let Joey personally answer them in this 4-set DVD compilation! Learn how to ensure the viability of your residence or workplace, Feng Shui-wise, without having to convert it into a Chinese antiques' shop. Classical Feng Shui is about harnessing the natural power of your environment to improve quality of life. It's a systematic and subtle metaphysical science.

And that's not all. Joey also debunks many a myth about classical Feng Shui, and shares with viewers Face Reading tips as well!

Own the series that national channel 8TV did a re-run of in 2005, today!

Feng Shui for Homebuyers Series

Feng Shui For Homebuyers - Exterior

Best selling Author and international Feng Shui Consultant, Joey Yap, will guide you on the various important features in your external environment that have a bearing on the Feng Shui of your home. For homeowners, those looking to build their own home or even investors who are looking to apply Feng Shui to their homes, this book provides valuable information from the classical Feng Shui theories and applications.

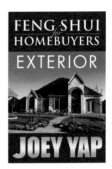

This book will assist you in screening and eliminating unsuitable options with negative FSQ (Feng Shui Quotient) should you acquire your own land or if you are purchasing a newly built home. It will also help you in determining which plot of land to select and which to avoid when purchasing an empty parcel of land.

Feng Shui for Homebuyers - Interior

A book every homeowner or potential house buyer should have. The Feng Shui for Homebuyers (Interior) is an informative reference book and invaluable guide written by best selling Author and international Feng Shui Consultant, Joey Yap.

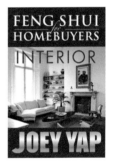

This book provides answers to the important questions of what really does matter when looking at the internal Feng Shui of a home or office. It teaches you how to analyze your home or office floor plans and how to improve their Feng Shui. It will answer all your questions about the positive and negative flow of Qi within your home and ways to utilize them to your maximum benefit.

Providing you with a guide to calculating your Life Gua and House Gua to fine-tune your Feng Shui within your property, Joey Yap focuses on practical, easily applicable ideas on what you can implement internally in a property.

Feng Shui for Apartment Buyers - Home Owners

Finding a good apartment or condominium is never an easy task but who do you ensure that is also has good Feng Shui? And how exactly do you apply Feng Shui to an apartment or condominium or high-rise residence?

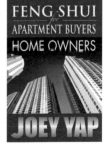

These questions and more are answered by renowned Feng Shui Consultant and Master Trainer Joey Yap in **Feng Shui for Apartment Buyers - Home Owners**. Joey answers the key questions about Feng Shui and apartments, then guides you through the bare basics like taking a direction and super-imposing a Flying Stars chart onto a floor plan. Joey also walks you through the process of finding an apartment with favorable Feng Shui, sharing with you some of the key methods and techniques that are employed by professional Feng Shui consultants in assesing apartment Feng Shui.

In his trademark straight-to-the-point manner, Joey shares with you the Feng Shui do's and dont's when it comes to finding an apartment with favorable Feng Shui and which is conducive for home living.

Educational Tools & Software

Mini Feng Shui Compass

This Mini Feng Shui Compass with the accompanying Companion Booklet written by leading Feng Shui and Chinese Astrology Master Trainer Joey Yap is a must-have for any Feng Shui enthusiast.

The Mini Feng Shui Compass is a self-aligning compass that is not only light at 100gms but also built sturdily to ensure it will be convenient to use anywhere. The rings on the Mini Feng Shui Compass are bi-lingual and incorporate the 24 Mountain Rings that is used in your traditional Luo Pan.

The comprehensive booklet included will guide you in applying the 24 Mountain Directions on your Mini Feng Shui Compass effectively and the 8 Mansions Feng Shui to locate the most auspicious locations within your home, office and surroundings. You can also use the Mini Feng Shui Compass when measuring the direction of your property for the purpose of applying Flying Stars Feng Shui.

BaZi Ming Pan Software Version 2.0
Professional Four Pillars Calculator for Destiny Analysis

The BaZi Ming Pan Version 2.0 Professional Four Pillars Calculator for Destiny Analysis is the most technically advanced software of its kind in the world today. It allows even those without any knowledge of BaZi to generate their own BaZi Charts, and provides virtually every detail required to undertake a comprehensive Destiny Analysis.

This Professional Four Pillars Calculator allows you to even undertake a day-to-day analysis of your Destiny. What's more, all BaZi Charts generated by this software are fully printable and configurable! Designed for both enthusiasts and professional practitioners, this state-of-the-art software blends details with simplicity, and is capable of generating 4 different types of BaZi charts: **BaZi Professional Charts, BaZi Annual Analysis Charts, BaZi Pillar Analysis Charts and BaZi Family Relationship Charts.**

Additional references, configurable to cater to all levels of BaZi knowledge and usage, include: • Dual Age & Bilingual Option (Western & Chinese) • Na Yin narrations • 12 Life Stages evaluation • Death & Emptiness • Gods & Killings • Special Days • Heavenly Virtue Nobles

This software also comes with a Client Management feature that allows you to save and trace clients' records instantly, navigate effortlessly between BaZi charts, and file your clients' information in an organized manner.

The BaZi Ming Pan Version 2.0 Calculator sets a new standard by combining the best of BaZi and technology.

Accelerate Your Face Reading Skills With Joey Yap's Face Reading Revealed DVD Series

Mian Xiang, the Chinese art of Face Reading, is an ancient form of physiognomy and entails the use of the face and facial characteristics to evaluate key aspects of a person's life, luck and destiny. In his Face Reading DVDs series, Joey Yap shows you how the facial features reveal a wealth of information about a person's luck, destiny and personality.

Mian Xiang also tell us the talents, quirks and personality of an individual. Do you know that just by looking at a person's face, you can ascertain his or her health, wealth, relationships and career? Let Joey Yap show you how the 12 Palaces can be utilised to reveal a person's inner talents, characteristics and much more.

Each facial feature on the face represents one year in a person's life. Your face is a 100-year map of your life and each position reveals your fortune and destiny at a particular age as well as insights and information about your personality, skills, abilities and destiny.

Using Mian Xiang, you will also be able to plan your life ahead by identifying, for example, the right business partner and knowing the sort of person that you need to avoid. By knowing their characteristics through the facial features, you will be able to gauge their intentions and gain an upper hand in negotiations.

Do you know what moles signify? Do they bring good or bad luck? Do you want to build better relationships with your partner or family members or have your ever wondered why you seem to be always bogged down by trivial problems in your life?

In these highly entertaining DVDs, Joey will help you answer all these questions and more. You will be able to ascertain the underlying meaning of moles, birthmarks or even the type of your hair in Face Reading. Joey will also reveal the guidelines to help you foster better and stronger relationships with your loved ones through Mian Xiang.

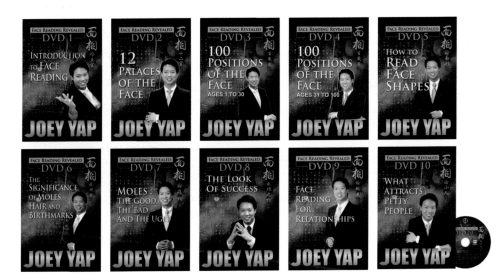

Continue Your Journey with Joey Yap's Books

BaZi - The Destiny Code (English & Chinese versions)

Leading Chinese Astrology Master Trainer Joey Yap makes it easy to learn how to unlock your Destiny through your BaZi with this book. BaZi or Four Pillars of Destiny is an ancient Chinese science which enables individuals to understand their personality, hidden talents and abilities as well as their luck cycle, simply by examining the information contained within their birth data. The Destiny Code is the first book that shows readers how to plot and interpret their own Destiny Charts and lays the foundation for more in-depth BaZi studies. Written in a lively entertaining style, the Destiny Code makes BaZi accessible to the layperson. Within 10 chapters, understand and appreciate more about this astoundingly accurate ancient Chinese Metaphysical science.

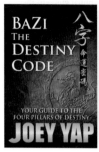

BaZi - The Destiny Code Revealed

In this follow up to Joey Yap's best-selling The Destiny Code, delve deeper into your own Destiny chart through an understanding of the key elemental relationships that affect the Heavenly Stems and Earthly Branches. Find out how Combinations, Clash, Harm, Destructions and Punishments bring new dimension to a BaZi chart. Complemented by extensive real-life examples, The Destiny Code Revealed takes you to the next level of BaZi, showing you how to unlock the Codes of Destiny and to take decisive action at the right time, and capitalise on the opportunities in life.

The Ten Thousand Year Calendar

The Ten Thousand Year Calendar or 萬年曆 Wan Nian Li is a regular reference book and an invaluable tool used by masters, practitioners and students of Feng Shui, BaZi (Four Pillars of Destiny), Chinese Zi Wei Dou Shu Astrology (Purple Star), Yi Jing (I-Ching) and Date Selection specialists.

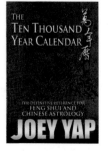

JOEY YAP's Ten Thousand Year Calendar provides the Gregorian (Western) dates converted into both the Chinese Solar and Lunar calendar in both the English and Chinese language.

It also includes a comprehensive set of key Feng Shui and Chinese Astrology charts and references, including Xuan Kong Nine Palace Flying Star Charts, Monthly and Daily Flying Stars, Water Dragon Formulas Reference Charts, Zi Wei Dou Shu (Purple Star) Astrology Reference Charts, BaZi (Four Pillars of Destiny) Heavenly Stems, Earthly Branches and all other related reference tables for Chinese Metaphysical Studies.

Annual Releases

Chinese Astrology for 2008

This information-packed annual guide to the Chinese Astrology for 2008 goes way beyond the conventional `animal horoscope' book. To begin with, author Joey Yap includes a personalized outlook for 2008 based on the individual's BaZi Day Pillar (Jia Zi) and a 12-month micro-analysis for each of the 60 Day Pillars – in addition to the annual outlook for all 12 animal signs and the 12-month outlook for each animal sign in 2008. Find out what awaits you in 2008 from the four key aspects of Health, Wealth, Career and Relationships… with Joey Yap's **Chinese Astrology for 2008**!

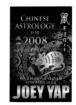

Feng Shui for 2008

Maximize the Qi of the Year of the Earth Rat for your home and office, with Joey Yap's **Feng Shui for 2008** book. Learn how to tap into the positive sectors of the year, and avoid the negative ones and those with the Annual Afflictions, as well as ascertain how the annual Flying Stars affect your property by comparing them against the Eight Mansions (Ba Zhai) for 2008. Flying Stars enthusiasts will also find this book handy, as it includes the monthly Flying Stars charts for the year, accompanied by detailed commentaries on what sectors to use and avoid – to enable you to optimize your Academic, Relationships and Wealth Luck in 2008.

Tong Shu Diary 2008

Organize your professional and personal lives with the **Tong Shu Diary 2008**, with a twist… it also allows you to determine the most suitable dates on which you can undertake important activities and endeavors throughout the year! This compact Diary integrates the Chinese Solar and Lunar Calendars with the universal lingua franca of the Gregorian Calendar.

Tong Shu Monthly Planner 2008

Tailor-made for the Feng Shui or BaZi enthusiast in you, or even professional Chinese Metaphysics consultants who want a compact planner with useful information incorporated into it. In the **Tong Shu Monthly Planner 2008**, you will find the auspicious and inauspicious dates for the year marked out for you, alongside the most suitable activities to be undertaken on each day. As a bonus, there is also a reference section containing all the monthly Flying Stars charts and Annual Afflictions for 2008.

Tong Shu Desktop Calendar 2008

Get an instant snapshot of the suitable and unsuitable activities for each day of the Year of the Earth Rat, with the icons displayed on this lightweight Desktop Calendar. Elegantly presenting the details of the Chinese Solar Calendar in the form of the standard Gregorian one, the **Tong Shu Desktop Calendar 2008** is perfect for Chinese Metaphysics enthusiasts and practitioners alike. Whether it a business launching or meeting, ground breaking ceremony, travel or house-moving that you have in mind, this Calendar is designed to fulfill your information needs.

Tong Shu Year Planner 2008

This one-piece Planner presents you all the essential information you need for significant activities or endeavors…with just a quick glance! In a nutshell, it allows you to identify the favorable and unfavorable days, which will in turn enable you to schedule your year's activities so as to make the most of good days, and avoid the ill-effects brought about by inauspicious ones.

Continue Your Journey with Joey Yap's Books

Mian Xiang - Discover Face Reading

Need to identify a suitable business partner? How about understanding your staff or superiors better? Or even choosing a suitable spouse? These mind boggling questions can be answered in Joey Yap's introductory book to Face Reading titled *Mian Xiang – Discover Face Reading*. This book will help you discover the hidden secrets in a person's face.

Mian Xiang – Discover Face Reading is comprehensive book on all areas of Face Reading, covering some of the most important facial features, including the forehead, mouth, ears and even the philtrum above your lips. This book will help you analyse not just your Destiny but help you achieve your full potential and achieve life fulfillment.

Stories and Lessons on Feng Shui (English & Chinese versions)

Stories and Lessons on Feng Shui is a compilation of essays and stories written by leading Feng Shui and Chinese Astrology trainer and consultant Joey Yap about Feng Shui and Chinese Astrology.

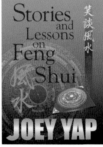

In this heart-warming collection of easy to read stories, find out why it's a myth that you should never have Water on the right hand side of your house, the truth behind the infamous 'love' and 'wealth' corners and that the sudden death of a pet fish is really NOT due to bad luck!

More Stories and Lessons on Feng Shui

Finally, the long-awaited sequel to *Stories & Lessons on Feng Shui*!

If you've read the best-selling Stories & Lessons on Feng Shui, you won't want to miss this book. And even if you haven't read *Stories & Lessons on Feng Shui*, there's always a time to rev your Feng Shui engine up.

The time is NOW.

And the book? *More Stories & Lessons on Feng Shui* – the 2nd compilation of the most popular articles and columns penned by Joey Yap; **specially featured in national and international publications, magazines and newspapers.**

All in all, *More Stories & Lessons on Feng Shui* is a delightful chronicle of Joey's articles, thoughts and vast experience - as a professional Feng Shui consultant and instructor - that have been purposely refined, edited and expanded upon to make for a light-hearted, interesting yet educational read. And with Feng Shui, BaZi, Mian Xiang and Yi Jing all thrown into this one dish, there's something for everyone...so all you need to serve or accompany *More Stories & Lessons on Feng Shui* with is your favorite cup of tea or coffee!

Continue Your Journey with Joey Yap's Books

Xuan Kong: Flying Stars Feng Shui

Xuan Kong Flying Stars Feng Shui is an essential introductory book to the subject of Xuan Kong Fei Xing, a well-known and popular system of Feng Shui, written by International Feng Shui Master Trainer Joey Yap.

In his down-to-earth, entertaining and easy to read style, Joey Yap takes you through the essential basics of Classical Feng Shui, and the key concepts of Xuan Kong Fei Xing (Flying Stars). Learn how to fly the stars, plot a Flying Star chart for your home or office and interpret the stars and star combinations. Find out how to utilise the favourable areas of your home or office for maximum benefit and learn 'tricks of the trade' and 'trade secrets' used by Feng Shui practitioners to enhance and maximise Qi in your home or office.

An essential integral introduction to the subject of Classical Feng Shui and the Flying Stars System of Feng Shui!

Xuan Kong Flying Stars: Structures and Combinations

Delve deeper into Flying Stars through a greater understanding of the 81 Combinations and the influence of the Annual and Monthly Stars on the Base, Sitting and Facing Stars in this 2nd book in the Xuan Kong Feng Shui series. Learn how Structures like the Combination of 10, Up the Mountain and Down the River, Pearl and Parent String Structures are used to interpret a Flying Star chart.

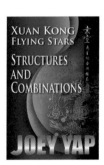

(Available in 2008)

Xuan Kong Flying Stars: Advanced Techniques

Take your knowledge of Xuan Kong Flying Stars to a higher level and learn how to apply complex techniques and advanced formulas such as Castle Gate Technique, Seven Star Robbery Formation, Advancing the Dragon Formation and Replacement Star technique amongst others. Joey Yap also shows you how to use the Life Palace technique to combine Gua Numbers with Flying Star numbers and utilise the predictive facets of Flying Stars Feng Shui.

(Available in 2009)

Continue Your Journey with Joey Yap's Books

The Art of Date Selection: Personal Date Selection

In today's modern world, it is not good enough to just do things effectively – we need to do them efficiently, as well. From the signing of business contracts and moving into a new home, to launching a product or even tying the knot; everything has to move, and move very quickly too. There is a premium on Time, where mistakes can indeed be costly.

The notion of doing the Right Thing, at the Right Time and in the Right Place is the very backbone of Date Selection. Because by selecting a suitable date specially tailored to a specific activity or endeavor, we infuse it with the most positive energies prevalent in our environment during that particular point in time; and that could well make the difference between `make-and-break'! With the *Art of Date Selection: Personal Date Selection*, learn simple, practical methods you can employ to select not just good dates, but personalized good dates. Whether it's a personal activity such as a marriage or professional endeavor such as launching a business, signing a contract or even acquiring assets, this book will show you how to pick the good dates and tailor them to suit the activity in question, as well as avoid the negative ones too!

The Art of Date Selection: Feng Shui Date Selection

Date Selection is the Art of selecting the most suitable date, where the energies present on the day support the specific activities or endeavors we choose to undertake on that day. Feng Shui is the Chinese Metaphysical study of the Physiognomy of the Land – landforms and the Qi they produce, circulate and conduct. Hence, anything that exists on this Earth is invariably subject to the laws of Feng Shui. So what do we get when Date Selection and Feng Shui converge?

(Available in 2008)

Feng Shui Date Selection, of course! Say you wish to renovate your home, or maybe buy or rent one. Or perhaps, you're a developer, and wish to know WHEN is the best date possible to commence construction works on your project. In any case – and all cases – you certainly wish to ensure that your endeavors are well supported by the positive energies present on a good day, won't you? And this is where Date Selection supplements the practice of Feng Shui. At the end of the day, it's all about making the most of what's good, and minimizing what's bad.

Elevate Your Feng Shui Skills With Joey Yap's Home Study Course And Educational DVDs

Xuan Kong Vol.1
An Advanced Feng Shui Home Study Course

Learn the Xuan Kong Flying Star Feng Shui system in just 20 lessons! Joey Yap's specialised notes and course work have been written to enable distance learning without compromising on the breadth or quality of the syllabus. Learn at your own pace with the same material students in a live class would use. The most comprehensive distance learning course on Xuan Kong Flying Star Feng Shui in the market. Xuan Kong Flying Star Vol.1 comes complete with a special binder for all your course notes.

Feng Shui for Period 8 - (DVD)

Don't miss the Feng Shui Event of the next 20 years! Catch Joey Yap LIVE and find out just what Period 8 is all about. This DVD boxed set zips you through the fundamentals of Feng Shui and the impact of this important change in the Feng Shui calendar. Joey's entertaining, conversational style walks you through the key changes that Period 8 will bring and how to tap into Wealth Qi and Good Feng Shui for the next 20 years.

Xuan Kong Flying Stars Beginners Workshop - (DVD)

Take a front row seat in Joey Yap's Xuan Kong Flying Stars workshop with this unique LIVE RECORDING of Joey Yap's Xuan Kong Flying Stars Feng Shui workshop, attended by over 500 people. This DVD program provides an effective and quick introduction of Xuan Kong Feng Shui essentials for those who are just starting out in their study of classical Feng Shui. Learn to plot your own Flying Star chart in just 3 hours. Learn 'trade secret' methods, remedies and cures for Flying Stars Feng Shui. This boxed set contains 3 DVDs and 1 workbook with notes and charts for reference.

BaZi Four Pillars of Destiny Beginners Workshop - (DVD)

Ever wondered what Destiny has in store for you? Or curious to know how you can learn more about your personality and inner talents? BaZi or Four Pillars of Destiny is an ancient Chinese science that enables us to understand a person's hidden talent, inner potential, personality, health and wealth luck from just their birth data. This specially compiled DVD set of Joey Yap's BaZi Beginners Workshop provides a thorough and comprehensive introduction to BaZi. Learn how to read your own chart and understand your own luck cycle. This boxed set contains 3 DVDs and 1 workbook with notes and reference charts.

Interested in learning MORE about Feng Shui? Advance Your Feng Shui Knowledge with the Mastery Academy Courses.

Feng Shui Mastery Series™
LIVE COURSES (MODULES ONE TO FOUR)

Feng Shui Mastery – Module One
Beginners Course

Designed for students seeking an entry-level intensive program into the study of Feng Shui , Module One is an intensive foundation course that aims not only to provide you with an introduction to Feng Shui theories and formulas and equip you with the skills and judgments to begin practicing and conduct simple Feng Shui audits upon successful completion of the course. Learn all about Forms, Eight Mansions Feng Shui and Flying Star Feng Shui in just one day with a unique, structured learning program that makes learning Feng Shui quick and easy!

Feng Shui Mastery – Module Two
Practitioners Course

Building on the knowledge and foundation in classical Feng Shui theory garnered in M1, M2 provides a more advanced and in-depth understanding of Eight Mansions, Xuan Kong Flying Star and San He and introduces students to theories that are found only in the classical Chinese Feng Shui texts. This 3-Day Intensive course hones analytical and judgment skills, refines Luo Pan (Chinese Feng Shui compass) skills and reveals 'trade secret' remedies. Module Two covers advanced Forms Analysis, San He's Five Ghost Carry Treasure formula, Advanced Eight Mansions and Xuan Kong Flying Stars and equips you with the skills needed to undertake audits and consultations for residences and offices.

Feng Shui Mastery – Module Three
Advanced Practitioners Course

Module Three is designed for Professional Feng Shui Practitioners. Learn advanced topics in Feng Shui and take your skills to a cutting edge level. Be equipped with the knowledge, techniques and confidence to conduct large scale audits (like estate and resort planning). Learn how to apply different systems appropriately to remedy situations or cases deemed inauspicious by one system and reconcile conflicts in different systems of Feng Shui. Gain advanced knowledge of San He (Three Harmony) systems and San Yuan (Three Cycles) systems, advanced Luan Tou (Forms Feng Shui) and specialist Water Formulas.

Feng Shui Mastery – Module Four
Master Course

The graduating course of the Feng Shui Mastery (FSM) Series, this course takes the advanced practitioner to the Master level. Power packed M4 trains students to 'walk the mountains' and identify superior landform, superior grade structures and make qualitative evaluations of landform, structures, Water and Qi and covers advanced and exclusive topics of San He, San Yuan, Xuan Kong, Ba Zhai, Luan Tou (Advanced Forms and Water Formula) Feng Shui. Master Internal, External and Luan Tou (Landform) Feng Shui methodologies to apply Feng Shui at every level and undertake consultations of every scale and magnitude, from houses and apartments to housing estates, townships, shopping malls and commercial districts.

BaZi Mastery Series™
LIVE COURSES (MODULES ONE TO FOUR)

BaZi Mastery – Module One
Intensive Foundation Course

This Intensive One Day Foundation Course provides an introduction to the principles and fundamentals of BaZi (Four Pillars of Destiny) and Destiny Analysis methods such as Ten Gods, Useful God and Strength of Qi. Learn how to plot a BaZi chart and interpret your Destiny and your potential. Master BaZi and learn to capitalize on your strengths, minimize risks and downturns and take charge of your Destiny.

BaZi Mastery – Module Two
Practical BaZi Applications

BaZi Module Two teaches students advanced BaZi analysis techniques and specific analysis methods for relationship luck, health evaluation, wealth potential and career potential. Students will learn to identify BaZi chart structures, sophisticated methods for applying the Ten Gods, and how to read Auxiliary Stars. Students who have completed Module Two will be able to conduct professional BaZi readings.

BaZi Mastery – Module Three
Advanced Practitioners Program

Designed for the BaZi practitioner, learn how to read complex cases and unique events in BaZi charts and perform Big and Small assessments. Discover how to analyze personalities and evaluate talents precisely, as well as special formulas and classical methodologies for BaZi from classics such as Di Tian Sui and Qiong Tong Bao Jian.

BaZi Mastery – Module Four
Master Course in BaZi

The graduating course of the BaZi Mastery Series, this course takes the advanced practitioner to the Masters' level. BaZi M4 focuses on specialized techniques of BaZi reading, unique special structures and advance methods from ancient classical texts. This program includes techniques on date selection and ancient methodologies from the Qiong Tong Bao Jian and Yuan Hai Zi Ping classics.

XUAN KONG MASTERY SERIES™
LIVE COURSES (MODULES ONE TO THREE)
* Advanced Courses For Master Practitioners

Xuan Kong Mastery – Module One
Advanced Foundation Program

This course is for the experienced Feng Shui professionals who wish to expand their knowledge and skills in the Xuan Kong system of Feng Shui, covering important foundation methods and techniques from the Wu Chang and Guang Dong lineages of Xuan Kong Feng Shui.

Xuan Kong Mastery – Module Two A
Advanced Xuan Kong Methodologies

Designed for Feng Shui practitioners seeking to specialise in the Xuan Kong system, this program focuses on methods of application and Joey Yap's unique Life Palace and Shifting Palace Methods, as well as methods and techniques from the Wu Chang lineage.

Xuan Kong Mastery – Module Two B
Purple White

Explore in detail and in great depth the star combinations in Xuan Kong. Learn how each different combination reacts or responds in different palaces, under different environmental circumstances and to whom in the property. Learn methods, theories and techniques extracted from ancient classics such as Xuan Kong Mi Zhi, Xuan Kong Fu, Fei Xing Fu and Zi Bai Jue.

Xuan Kong Mastery – Module Three
Advanced Xuan Kong Da Gua

This intensive course focuses solely on the Xuan Kong Da Gua system covering the theories, techniques and methods of application of this unique 64-Hexagram based system of Xuan Kong including Xuan Kong Da Gua for landform analysis.

Mian Xiang Mastery Series™
LIVE COURSES (MODULES ONE AND TWO)

Mian Xiang Mastery – Module One
Basic Face Reading

A person's face is their fortune – learn more about the ancient Chinese art of Face Reading. In just one day, be equipped with techniques and skills to read a person's face and ascertain their character, luck, wealth and relationship luck.

Mian Xiang Mastery – Module Two
Practical Face Reading

Mian Xiang Module Two covers face reading techniques extracted from the ancient classics Shen Xiang Quan Pian and Shen Xiang Tie Guan Dau. Gain a greater depth and understanding of Mian Xiang and learn to recognize key structures and characteristics in a person's face.

Yi Jing Mastery Series™
LIVE COURSES (MODULES ONE AND TWO)

Yi Jing Mastery – Module One
Traditional Yi Jing

'Yi', relates to change. Change is the only constant in life and the universe, without exception to this rule. The Yi Jing is hence popularly referred to as the Book or Classic of Change. Discoursed in the language of Yin and Yang, the Yi Jing is one of the oldest Chinese classical texts surviving today. With Traditional Yi Jing, learnn how this Classic is used to divine the outcomes of virtually every facet of life; from your relationships to seeking an answer to the issues you may face in your daily life.

Yi Jing Mastery – Module Two
Plum Blossom Numerology

Shao Yong, widely regarded as one of the greatest scholars of the Sung Dynasty, developed Mei Hua Yi Shu (Plum Blossom Numerology) as a more advanced means for divination purpose using the Yi Jing. In Plum Blossom Numerology, the results of a hexagram are interpreted by referring to the Gua meanings, where the interaction and relationship between the five elements, stems, branches and time are equally taken into consideration. This divination method, properly applied, allows us to make proper decisions whenever we find ourselves in a predicament.

Ze Ri Mastery Series™
LIVE COURSES (MODULES ONE AND TWO)

Ze Ri Mastery Series Module 1
Personal and Feng Shui Date Selection

The Mastery Academy's Date Selection Mastery Series Module 1 is specifically structured to provide novice students with an exciting introduction to the Art of Date Selection. Learn the rudiments and tenets of this intriguing metaphysical science. What makes a good date, and what makes a bad date? What dates are suitable for which activities, and what dates simply aren't? And of course, the mother of all questions: WHY aren't all dates created equal. All in only one Module – Module 1!

Ze Ri Mastery Series Module 2
Xuan Kong Da Gua Date Selection

In Module 2, discover advanced Date Selection techniques that will take your knowledge of this Art to a level equivalent to that of a professional's! This is the Module where Date Selection infuses knowledge of the ancient metaphysical science of Feng Shui and BaZi (Chinese Astrology, or Four Pillars of Destiny). Feng Shui, as a means of maximizing Human Luck (i.e. our luck on Earth), is often quoted as the cure to BaZi, which allows us to decipher our Heaven (i.e. inherent) Luck. And one of the most potent ways of making the most of what life has to offer us is to understand our Destiny, know how we can use the natural energies of our environment for our environments and MOST importantly, WHEN we should use these energies and for WHAT endeavors!

You will learn specific methods on how to select suitable dates, tailored to specific activities and events. More importantly, you will also be taught how to suit dates to a person's BaZi (Chinese Astrology, or Four Pillars of Destiny), in order to maximize his or her strengths, and allow this person to surmount any challenges that lie in wait. Add in the factor of `place', and you would have satisfied the notion of `doing the right thing, at the right time and in the right place'! A basic knowledge of BaZi and Feng Shui will come in handy in this Module, although these are not pre-requisites to successfully undergo Module 2.

Walk the Mountains! Learn Feng Shui in a
Practical and Hands-on Program

Feng Shui Mastery Excursion Series™ : CHINA

Learn landform (Luan Tou) Feng Shui by walking the mountains and chasing the Dragon's vein in China. This Program takes the students in a study tour to examine notable Feng Shui landmarks, mountains, hills, valleys, ancient palaces, famous mansions, houses and tombs in China. The Excursion is a 'practical' hands-on course where students are shown to perform readings using the formulas they've learnt and to recognize and read Feng Shui Landform (Luan Tou) formations.

Read about China Excursion here:
http://www.masteryacademy.com/Education/schoolfengshui/fengshuimasteryexcursion.asp

---

Mastery Academy courses are conducted around the world. Find out when will Joey Yap be in your area by visiting **www.masteryacademy.com** or call our office at **+603-2284 8080**.